What People Are Saying About Wild Women Throw a Party!

Lynette Shirk's recipes rival any four-star restaurant—she is a true goddess in the kitchen and has concocted a guide to throwing the coolest parties ever!

—**Margie Lapanja**, author of *Romancing the Stove* and *Food Men Love*

Take one part great food and mix with two parts Silver Screen Sirens and what do you get? *Wild Women Throw a Party*, the best party book in the entire world!

—**Tim Wright**, author of *Raging Beauties*

Here's another way to be a wild woman: eat like one! Politicos can sip soup with Eleanor Roosevelt. Literary ladies, born too late to sit at the Algonquin Round Table? You can still share wine and cheese with Edna St. Vincent Millay or have cocktails with Dorothy Parker (but don't drink too much!). Or lace up those ballet shoes, dance on the table with Zelda Fitzgerald, but don't knock over the Waldorf salad. Lynette Rohrer Shirk supplies the recipes, you throw the party.

—**Trina Robbins**, author of *Wild Irish Roses* and *Tender Murderers*

"Once, I was at a party Lynette was throwing and found myself in a hot tub with a rock band. But, all I could think about was the platter of Pigs in a Blanket she was serving. That is how great her recipes are!"

—**Varla Ventura**, author of *Wild Women Talk About Love* and *Sheroes*

Wild Women Throw a Party

110 Original Recipes and Amazing Menus for Birthday Bashes, Power Showers, Poker Soirees, and Celebrations Galore

Lynette Rohrer Shirk

Foreword by Ame Mahler Beanland

Conari Press

For Zelda

First published in 2007 by Conari Press,
an imprint of Red Wheel/Weiser, LLC
With offices at:
500 Third Street, Suite 230
San Francisco, CA 94107
www.redwheelweiser.com

ISBN-10: 1-57324-284-5
ISBN-13: 978-1-57324-284-4

Library of Congress Cataloging-in-Publication Data
Shirk, Lynette Rohrer.
Wild women throw a party : 110 original recipes and amazing menus for birthday bashes, power
showers, poker soirees, and celebrations galore/Lynette Rohrer Shirk.
      p. cm.
Includes bibliographical references and index.
ISBN 1-57324-284-5 (alk. paper)
1. Entertaining. 2. Menus. 3. Parties. I. Title.
TX731.S4543 2007
642'.4—dc22
                                    2006034322

Cover and interior design by Maija Tollefson.

Cover and interior photographs © Corbis Images.

Printed in Canada

TCP

10 9 8 7 6 5 4 3 2 1

The paper used in this publication meets the minimum requirements of the American National Standard for Information
 Sciences-Permanence of Paper for Printed Library Materials Z39.48-1992 (R1997).

Contents

Foreword

The best party advice I ever received came from two of the most fabulous wild women I have ever known. The first was from the beloved Sweet Potato Queen Jill Conner Browne who swears that you should "never wear panties to a party." The other is from Lynette Rohrer Shirk, author of this book and a co-author of the fabulous *Wild Women in the Kitchen*, who wisely told me: "Always make sure the cooking wine is good enough to drink." Once you know what to wear (or not) and what to drink (or not), the only things you need to get the party started are some trusty recipes and a shot of inspiration. That's where *Wild Women Throw a Party* comes in.

This book is the ultimate good-time muse. With its sassy attitude, iron-clad recipes, and inspiring themes, it never fails to get me excited about planning a get-together. With parties like Peggy Guggenheim's Art Gallery Opening, Dorothy Parker's Cocktail Party, and Women of the Senate Poker Party to guide you, you'll be sure to offer an experience that's as intellectually and creatively stimulating as it is fabulously fun and delicious.

Forget polishing the silver, timing the soufflé perfectly and mastering napkin origami. In this book, Lynette shares something that other cookbooks and entertaining books fail to understand—the best soirées do not spring from overly orchestrated labor or insane attention to detail. Good parties—great parties—spring wildly from unexpected combinations of interesting conversation, festive spirits, and delicious food simply prepared.

While *Wild Women Throw a Party* bursts with attitude and joie de vivre, make no bones about it, Lynette is no slouch in the technique department. She's got all the snooty qualifications—world-class culinary training, 5-star restaurant experience, legions of A-list and celebrity fans—without any of the "I can cook better than you" condescension. Lynette appreciates a fine, hand-made French cheese, but you'll be just as likely to find a stick of Velveeta in her cupboard. And with her help you could make something delicious out of either.

With Lynette's easy-to-follow methods and down-to-earth voice, *Wild Women Throw a Party* is like cooking alongside your best girlfriend with a glass of wine and an 80s mix tape playing in the background. She makes entertaining feel the way it should—effortless and fun.

I confess that for my endorsement of this book, I was buttered up. Wild women know how to get what they want and in this case Lynette knew exactly how to curry my favor. I was plied with irresistible creations—dinner plate-sized almond torte cookies frosted in bittersweet chocolate, melt-in-your-mouth sugar cookies, and homemade nut brittle spiked with coffee beans, to name just a few of the treats that secured my commendations.

—Ame Mahler Beanland

In the Beginning, There Were Wild Women

This celebration of Wild Women is more than just another cookbook; it is a book full of women's history, stories, biographies, party themes, recipes, ideas, inspirations, tidbits of information, and fun. Wild Women of notoriety are explored, explained, and paired with a party theme and recipes related to their unique stories. Sophia Loren's Pajama Party is a tribute to the diet of pasta that created a legend. Joan Crawford's Mother's Day dishes about the actress and her eccentricities while dishing out such recipes as What Ever Happened to Baby Back Ribs and Mildred Pierce's Roast Chicken. The Women of the Senate's Poker Party lets you know when to hold 'em and Dorothy Parker's Cocktail Party will help you pretend the Volstead Act never passed! The darker side of Wild Women is exposed in *The Bacchae* Halloween Party, complete with omo- phagia (raw flesh-eating); and murder and obsession are entangled with a famous turn-of-the-century restaurant in A Florodora Girl's After-Hours Dinner Party. Occasions include the Oscars, New Year's Eve, Mardi Gras, and Halloween while a Picnic, a Pool Party, or an Ice Cream Social are themes to celebrate any occasion such as a birthday, holiday, or shower. You can turn anything into an occasion to celebrate, with the right attitude and a few great recipes. Here's a recipe the original Wild Woman (Eve) could have used to throw a garden party with her fig leaves; and one hundred more party-worthy recipes.

Original Sin Halibut

SERVES 2

INGREDIENTS:

2 large fig leaves

2 six ounce filets of halibut

1 teaspoon olive oil

   salt and pepper to taste

METHOD:

1.   Preheat oven to 350 degrees F.

2.   Wipe fig leaves clean with a damp towel.

3.   Dip fingers in olive oil and smooth some on each fig leaf.

4.   Sprinkle the halibut filets with salt and pepper and place one on each fig leaf.

5.   Fold and tuck the sides of the fig leaf up and around the halibut and place the packet seam side down on an oiled baking sheet so the leaves don't unwrap.

6.   Bake for 15 minutes.

7.   Remove from the oven and turn the packets over. Carefully open the leaves and transfer the halibut to plates.

Chapter 1

Party Girls

The Mistress of Modernism's Art Gallery Opening

Peggy Guggenheim

Peggy Guggenheim was a twentieth-century patroness of the arts, most notable for bringing together the European Surrealists with the American Abstract Expressionists. She opened her New York Gallery, Art of This Century, in December 1942. A partial inventory of the opening works includes pieces by Arp, Brancusi, Calder, Chagall, Duchamp, Ernst, Kandinsky, Klee, Magritte, Man Ray, Miro, Mondrian, Picasso, and Vail (her first husband).

Art of This Century was comparable to the Armory Show of 1913, with its scandalous modern content that rocked popular imagination and drew large crowds. Peggy's gallery was interactive, making art fun and accessible to a general audience rather than just to elite wealthy buyers. It was a highly democratic experience, with the idea that it would be an art center where ideas would be freely exchanged. Its goal was to show that art was not static. The mission of the gallery was to serve the future, not to record the past, and its greatest contribution was that it showed unproven artists.

Peggy Guggenheim was one of only two female gallery owners in New York at the time of opening Art of This Century. She exhibited an all-women's art show, "Exhibition by 31 Women" in January 1943, with the works of Frida

Kahlo, Leonora Carrington, Gypsy Rose Lee, and Meret Oppenheim (who had shocked MOMA viewers with her fur-lined tea set). She has said that her single greatest discovery was Jackson Pollock, whose career she launched with a one-man show.

A Bohemian Painter's Party

Peggy Guggenheim's discovery, Jackson Pollock, is credited with the invention of "action painting." In action painting, Pollock used sticks instead of brushes to drip and fling paint onto a giant canvas, which was not upright on an easel but laid out flat on the floor of his barn studio. He hovered over the canvas and became part of the painting. The recipes below take off on the painting theme to create an artist's palette for your guests' palates!

The recipe for Paint "Brushes" with Paint Pot Dipping Sauces mimics Pollock's technique because the "brushes" have no brush, just the stick part. The different colored dipping sauces are arranged to resemble paint pots. The sauce flavors are honey-mustard, lemony ranch, zesty barbecue, olive-marinara and sesame-soy. The Modern Art Tart is an eggplant pizza with Asian flavors. It is garnished like an abstract modern art piece with various forms and vibrant colors. For dessert, the Jackson Pollock Ice Cream Canvases give your guests a chance to create their own paintings of vanilla ice cream with colorful sauces of caramel, butterscotch, chocolate, and strawberry. The Painter's Palette Cookies complete the meal and the theme with a sugar cookie cutout in the shape of a paint palette and painted with a mixture of egg yolk and food coloring. (Renaissance artists painted with a similar mixture of egg yolk and tempera pigment.)

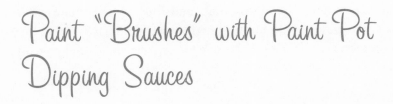

Paint "Brushes" with Paint Pot Dipping Sauces

SERVES 6

INGREDIENTS:

18 hard breadsticks

18 slices bacon

½ cup brown sugar

1 teaspoon ground cumin

¼ cup Dijon mustard

¼ cup honey

½ cup ranch dressing

1 tablespoon lemon juice

½ cup barbecue sauce

2 tablespoons Worcestershire sauce

½ teaspoon cayenne pepper sauce

½ cup marinara sauce

2 tablespoons chopped black olives

½ cup soy sauce

1 tablespoon sesame oil

1 tablespoon sliced green onions

METHOD:

1. Preheat oven to 350 degrees F. Line a baking sheet with foil and set aside.

2. Wrap each breadstick with a slice of bacon in a spiral so the bacon is wound around the breadstick from end to end.

3. Spread the brown sugar out on a piece of foil and sprinkle the cumin over it. Mix to combine with your fingers and gently squeeze out any lumps in the brown sugar.

4. Roll the bacon-wrapped breadsticks in the brown sugar mixture to lightly coat them and place them on the foil-lined baking sheet.

5. Bake for 20 minutes. Remove from the pan and cool on lettuce leaves (the grease can drain and they won't stick to lettuce like they would to paper towels.)

6. Combine the Dijon mustard and the honey for one dipping sauce.

7. Combine the ranch dressing and lemon juice for the second dipping sauce.

8. Combine the barbecue sauce with the Worcestershire sauce and cayenne pepper sauce for the third dipping sauce.

9. Combine the marinara sauce with the chopped black olives for the fourth dipping sauce.

10. Combine the soy sauce, sesame oil, and sliced green onions for the fifth dipping sauce.

11. Put the "brushes" in a cylindrical vessel, such as a vase or a clean paint bucket, and arrange the five dipping sauces in small bowls or ramekins around the brushes.

Modern Art Tart

SERVES 6

INGREDIENTS:

1 prebaked pizza shell

2 Japanese eggplants

¼ cup olive oil

   salt and pepper to taste

¼ cup roasted red bell pepper strips

½ cup hoisin sauce

¼ cup sliced green onions

¼ cup smoked Gouda cheese, shredded

2 tablespoons chopped peanuts

   fresh cilantro leaves

METHOD:

1. Preheat oven to 350 degrees F.

2. Slice eggplants into ¼-inch rounds and brush them with oil. Sprinkle them with salt and pepper and grill them on a grill pan or an outdoor grill. Be sure to cook them until they are tender enough to eat and try to get striped grill marks on them for flavor and presentation.

3. Put the pizza shell on a pizza pan and spread the hoisin sauce over it.

4. Arrange the grilled eggplant slices over the sauce, then scatter the roasted red bell pepper strips and sliced green onions over the eggplant. Sprinkle the cheese evenly over the tart.

5. Bake the tart for 15 minutes, until the cheese has melted and everything is heated through. Remove the tart from oven.

6. Garnish the tart with the chopped peanuts and fresh cilantro leaves and cut it into 6 wedges.

Jackson Pollock Ice Cream Canvases

SERVES 6

INGREDIENTS:

6 ounces cream

6 ounces chocolate chips

1 cup frozen, sweetened strawberries, thawed

½ cup caramel sauce

½ cup butterscotch sauce

1 rectangular block of vanilla ice cream (half-gallon)

4 plastic squeeze bottles

METHOD:

1. In a saucepan, heat the cream to a simmer. Add the chocolate chips and remove the pan from the heat. Let sit for 10 minutes, and then stir the melted chocolate into the cream to combine. Pour this chocolate sauce into a plastic squeeze bottle and keep in a warm place.

2. Purée the strawberries with their liquid in a blender and then strain it. Pour this strawberry sauce into a plastic squeeze bottle and set aside.

3. Heat the jars of caramel and butterscotch in a saucepan of warm water. Pour the sauces into two separate plastic squeeze bottles and keep in a warm place.

4. Peel the sides of the ice cream container down to expose the sides of the rectangular block of ice cream.

5. Cut the ice cream block, with a knife warmed in hot water, into 1– to 2–inch slices and place them on each guest's plate.

6. Set the squeeze bottles of sauces out for your guests to paint their own ice cream canvases à la Jackson Pollock.

Painter's Palette Cookies

Serves 12

Ingredients:

4 ounces soft butter

1 cup sugar

1 egg

1 tablespoon cream

½ teaspoon vanilla

½ teaspoon salt

1 teaspoon baking powder

1¾ cups flour

1 egg yolk

food coloring (red, blue, yellow)

Method:

1. Preheat oven to 300 degrees F.

2. In a mixing bowl with an electric mixer cream together butter and sugar until fluffy. Add egg, cream, and vanilla and mix well. Scrape down the sides of the bowl.

3. In a separate bowl mix together the salt, baking powder, and flour and then add the dry ingredients to the butter mixture. Mix to form a smooth dough.

continued

4. Roll out the dough on a lightly floured surface to prevent sticking. With a 3-inch x 4-inch oval or egg-shaped cookie cutter, cut cookies out of the dough. Brush excess flour off the cookies and place them on cookie sheets.

5. Cut a small off-center circle out of the cookie with a canapé cutter or the large end of a pastry piping tip to resemble the part of the palette that the thumb and brushes go through.

6. Divide the egg yolk, mix it with different colors of food coloring, and paint it on the cookies in circles around the edge to resemble the paint on a painter's palette.

7. Bake cookies for 12–15 minutes. Cool on a rack.

Proper Attire

Inform your guests on the invitation to wear or bring their own painting smocks because they will be creating their own edible artwork at the party. Suggest that they "brush up" on their knowledge of modern artists and hold a game of guess-the-artist by showing pictures of paintings with the artists' signatures covered. Award various art supplies, such as paints and brushes, for prizes.

Titanic Tragedy

In 1912 when Peggy was thirteen years old, her father,
Benjamin Guggenheim, brother of Solomon Guggenheim
of art museum fame, went down with the Titanic in full
evening attire. After his death, heiress Peggy was
thought of as the "poor relation" in the family.

The Queen of Palm Beach's Luncheon

Marjorie Merriweather Post

Marjorie Merriweather Post was the only daughter of breakfast food innovator C.W. Post. Her father's inventions include Postum, a coffee substitute, Grape-Nuts cereal, and Post Toasties breakfast flakes. Born in 1887 in Springfield, Illinois, Marjorie was involved at an early age in her father's entrepreneurial projects. As a child she glued Postum labels onto the product's packages and when her father moved the family to Battle Creek, Michigan, she accompanied him on sales trips to win shelf space in a Grand Rapids grocery store next to his fellow inventor and competitor Kellogg. After Postum's success came a ready-to-eat breakfast food that was touted as "Marjorie's Baby Food"—Grape-Nuts. Marjorie later made her own mark on the company her father started by purchasing Clarence Birdseye's "frosted foods" company, General Foods. She was sympathetic to the average housewife's drudgery in the kitchen even though she didn't cook herself, and she was determined to make a difference by providing them with convenient alternatives for preparing the family meals.

The heiress to the cereal fortune became the toast of Palm Beach society along with her second husband, E.F. Hutton, in the 1920s, a time when the stuffy Old Society was breaking down to make way for the Jazz Age's cult of youth. The virtues of hospitality and sociability from Marjorie's middle-class Midwestern childhood and her participation in her family's acts of charity to the ill and needy combined with her fortune to pave the way for the elaborate benefit balls she staged in Palm Beach. Marjorie, now the "Queen of Palm Beach," threw theme parties and costume parties with friends such as the flamboyant showman Flo Ziegfeld and his actress wife Billie Burke. In a tribute to those sophisticated soirees, here is a dinner menu suitable for entertaining your friends Palm Beach style.

A Cereal Queen's Party

This luncheon menu starts with a Cold Cucumber Soup that was once on the menu of one of Marjorie's friend Billie Burke's dinner parties. The dainty Palm Beach Finger Sandwiches are so called because a sandwich filled with pimento cheese is sometimes called a "Palm Beach." (The vintage Highland Park Pharmacy lunch counter in Dallas has it on their menu.) Macadamia Nut Crusted Trout is an elegant entrée and it happens to have one of Marjorie's pet projects in the ingredients: macadamia nuts. Ms. Post financed a cousin's idea to plant macadamia seedlings in Hawaii and made arrangements with General Electric to create a macadamia nutshell cracking machine. Before this, there was no macadamia nut industry.

For dessert, a nod to the breakfast cereal that made Marjorie Merriweather Post's ascendancy to the throne as the Queen of Palm Beach possible, Grape-Nuts Ice Cream.

Cold Cucumber Soup

SERVES 6

INGREDIENTS:

3 cucumbers

½ cup chicken broth

1 cup cream

  salt and peper to taste

2 slices smoked salmon

¼ cup sour cream

6 fresh dill sprigs

METHOD:

1.   Peel, seed, and chop the cucumbers.

2.   In a blender, purée the cucumbers with the chicken broth until smooth. Add the cream and blend again until smooth. Season with salt and pepper. Chill until ready to serve.

3.   Slice the smoked salmon into strips.

4.   Divide the cucumber soup evenly among 6 chilled soup bowls.

5.   Garnish each soup bowl with the smoked salmon strips, a dollop of sour cream, and a dill sprig.

Palm Beach Finger Sandwiches

SERVES 6

INGREDIENTS:

4 ounces sharp yellow cheddar cheese

4 ounces white cheddar cheese

¼ cup diced pimentos

1 tablespoon cream

¼ cup mayonnaise and
salt and pepper to taste

12 slices good white bread (thin slices)

METHOD:

1. Shred the yellow and white cheddar cheeses and put in a bowl.

2. Add the pimentos, cream, and mayonnaise to the cheese and mix well.

3. Season the pimento cheese mixture with salt and pepper.

4. Divide the pimento cheese among six slices of bread and spread it out.
   Top with the remaining six slices of bread to make sandwiches.

5. Cut the crusts off the sandwiches and discard them. (Or snack on them!)

6. Cut each crustless sandwich into four triangles and arrange them on a platter.

Macadamia Nut Crusted Trout

SERVES 6

INGREDIENTS:

3 whole rainbow trout, deboned
    salt and pepper to taste
¾ cup chopped macadamia nuts

¾ cup bread crumbs
½ cup melted butter
6 lemon wedges

METHOD:

1. Preheat oven to 400 degrees F. Open up the fish and then place, skin side down, on an oiled baking tray. Season them with salt and pepper.

2. Combine the macadamia nuts with bread crumbs and coat the fish flesh with the mixture.

3. Drizzle the melted butter over the macadamia nut crust.

4. Bake the trout for 12 minutes, and then broil it to brown the crust.

5. Serve with lemon wedges to squeeze on top.

Grape-Nuts Ice Cream

SERVES 6

SERVES 6

INGREDIENTS:

1 cup half-and-half	1 cup cream
⅔ cup sugar	1 tablespoon vanilla
4 egg yolks	½ cup Grape-Nuts cereal

METHOD:

1. Heat the half-and-half and the sugar to a simmer, then turn the heat to low.

2. In a bowl, beat the egg yolks with a whisk to break them up and then temper them with ½ cup of the hot half-and-half.

3. Pour the egg yolk mixture into the rest of the heated half-and-half and cook, stirring constantly, until the custard thickens to coat the back of a spoon. Remove from heat.

4. Immediately strain the hot custard into a bowl set in an ice bath.

5. Stir the cream and vanilla into the custard and let the mixture chill completely, stirring occasionally to let the steam escape.

continued

6. Freeze the chilled ice cream custard in an ice cream maker according to manufacturer's instructions.

7. Add the Grape-Nuts when the ice cream is almost finished. Store in the freezer until ready to serve.

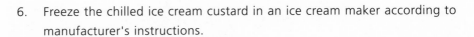

Mar-A-Lago

Marjorie Merriweather Post and E.F. Hutton built this Palm Beach Florida palace at the height of the Roaring Twenties on seventeen acres between Lake Worth and the Atlantic Ocean. Designed by the Ziegfeld Follies stage set designer, Mar-A-Lago was elaborately decorated with furniture, tapestries, and paintings from decaying ducal palaces. The estate was the site for Marjorie's elaborate benefit galas where she and her hundreds of glittering guests would party the night away under an artificial blue moon. Mar-A-Lago is now owned by Donald Trump.

The Original Flapper's Hotel Room Fete

Zelda Sayre Fitzgerald

Zelda Fitzgerald was born to party. She set the standard for the Jazz Age cult of youth in the 1920s, dazzling society with her unbridled spirit and fearlessness. Even before she was a wild woman she was a wild child. Growing up in Montgomery, Alabama, she acted on her impulses regardless of what other people thought. She swam in a scandalous flesh-colored bathing suit, hung out at the ice cream parlor sipping dopes instead of doing her homework, and wore mascara before the other girls did. She was no proper Southern belle! Zelda Sayre's fiery personality attracted the attention of F. Scott Fitzgerald at a country club dance when he was an Army officer stationed near her home town during World War I. It was love at first sight for both of them. After a rocky courtship, Zelda and Scott were married in New York City in the spring of 1920 and began living the high life in peerless fashion. They took up residence in the Biltmore Hotel and regularly ordered fresh spinach and Champagne for midnight snacks.

The Fitzgeralds never lived in one place for very long. They rented a cottage in Westport, Connecticut, and continued to party with friends from New York before moving back to Manhattan. They retreated to St. Paul, Minnesota (Scott's family home) for the birth of their daughter, and then they rented a house in Great Neck, New York, where they partied with their neighbor Ring Lardner. They went to Paris to take their place in café society, partying with Ernest Hemingway and other American expatriates, and then they rented a villa on the French Riviera where Zelda entertained herself by cliff diving into the sea and dancing on restaurant tables. They returned to the United States and after a stint in Hollywood, they rented an old mansion on the Delaware River where they could get some rest from their wild ways and Scott could get down to work.

Scott turned this rich life experience into his great American novel *The Great Gatsby* and several more, in addition to numerous short stories. Zelda was his muse and some of her ideas were infused in his stories, for example *The Jelly Bean*. His novels were inspired by the life he was living with Zelda but he claimed the material as his territory. Zelda tried to carve out a career of her own as a ballerina but became obsessed with this quest to the point of exhaustion. So she started competing with him in the literary world, writing a lengthy play, *Candalabra*, a novel, *Save Me the Waltz*, and short stories including *Eulogy on the Flapper*. Zelda also began painting and ultimately had an exhibition of her work in New York in 1934. The following party is a tribute to Zelda's arrival in Manhattan and the decadent hotel life the newly-wed Fitzgeralds shared at the dawn of the Jazz Age.

Room Service for a Party of Two

In honor of the salad days of Zelda and Scott, this intimate party is for lovers— lovers of romance and fancy hotels, champagne and room service. Stay in your bedroom all day watching movies and enjoying these dishes. My favorite thing to order from room service in a luxury hotel is breakfast in bed, and the recipes for Eggs Benedict and Hollandaise Sauce are classics of the genre. Waldorf Salad is suitable for a light lunch while you are lazing the day away in your "suite." This salad was named after the Waldorf-Astoria hotel, where it was invented in 1896. In homage to the spinach and Champagne the Fitzgeralds dined on at the Biltmore, Champagne Creamed Spinach combines both ingredients to make flapper-inspired ambrosia for your midnight pleasure.

Eggs Benedict

INGREDIENTS:

2 English muffins

1 tablespoon white vinegar

4 slices Canadian bacon

4 eggs

½ cup warm Hollandaise sauce
   (recipe follows)

2 black olives

METHOD:

1. Split the English muffins, wrap them in foil, and keep them in a warm oven until ready to assemble the Eggs Benedict.

2. Bring a saucepan full of water to a simmer and stir in the vinegar.

3. While the water is coming to a simmer, fry the Canadian bacon in a skillet, and then keep it in a warm place until ready to assemble the Eggs Benedict.

4. Crack the eggs individually into a teacup and gently slide them into the simmering vinegar water. Poach the eggs until the whites are set and the centers are still soft. Remove poached eggs from the simmering water with a slotted spoon and drain them on several layers of paper towels.

5. Remove the English muffins from the warm oven and open them. Place a piece of fried Canadian bacon on each muffin half and then top the Canadian bacon with a poached egg.

6. Spoon enough Hollandaise sauce onto each poached egg to cover.

7. Cut the black olives in half lengthwise and garnish each egg with one of the halves. Serve two eggs per person.

Hollandaise Sauce

SERVES 2

INGREDIENTS:

1 egg yolk

1½ teaspoons cold water

2 ounces melted butter

½ teaspoon lemon juice

pinch cayenne pepper

salt and white pepper to taste

METHOD:

1. Whisk egg yolk and water in a stainless steel or glass bowl over simmering water and cook until mixture thickens to ribbon stage.

continued

2. Slowly pour melted butter into yolks, drop by drop at first, whisking constantly to form an emulsion. Pour the butter in a thin stream after the emulsion gets started and the sauce starts to thicken, and continue whisking.

3. Remove bowl from heat and whisk in the lemon juice and cayenne pepper.

4. Season sauce with salt and white pepper to taste.

5. Serve immediately or keep in a warm but not too hot place until ready to serve. (A thermos will hold it at the perfect temperature for a long while.)

Waldorf Salad

SERVES 2

INGREDIENTS:

¼ cup cream

¼ cup mayonnaise

1 cup diced red apple

½ cup diced celery

¼ cup halved seedless grapes

¼ cup chopped pecans

1 teaspoon lemon juice

salt and pepper to taste

2 leaves butter lettuce

METHOD:

1. Whip the cream to soft peaks in a bowl. Whisk the mayonnaise into the whipped cream.

2. Add the apple, celery, grapes, and pecans to the mixture and fold every thing together.

3. Season the salad with the lemon juice and salt and pepper to taste.

4. Serve the chopped salad on a butter lettuce leaf.

Champagne Creamed Spinach

SERVES 2

INGREDIENTS:

2 ounces unsalted butter

1 minced garlic clove

6-ounce package, prewashed fresh
   baby spinach leaves

¼ cup Champagne

¼ cup cream

pinch of salt

2 pinches of white pepper

2 pinches of ground nutmeg

1 tablespoon grated Parmesan cheese

12 toast points

METHOD:

1. Preheat oven to 350 degrees F.

2. Melt butter in a 12-inch sauté pan and sweat the garlic in it for 2 minutes over medium heat.

3. Add all the spinach at once, then add the Champagne and cover the pan with a lid to steam for 5 minutes.

4. Lift the spinach out of the liquid in the pan with tongs and set it aside in a 12-ounce gratin dish.

5. Add the cream to the liquid left in the pan, turn the heat to high and reduce liquid by half, 5 minutes.

6. Sprinkle the salt, pepper, and nutmeg over the cream reduction and swirl the pan to distribute the seasonings. Remove the pan from heat.

7. Pour the cream reduction over the spinach in the gratin dish, sprinkle the spinach with the Parmesan cheese and bake for 15 minutes, until browned.

8. Serve with toast points.

Party in Shangri-La

Doris Duke

Born with a silver spoon in her mouth in 1912, Doris Duke would become
the heiress to her father's tobacco fortune at age twelve. Born to a rags-to-riches
millionaire, baby Doris grew up in an opulent Fifth Avenue mansion in New
York and immediately started receiving sacks of mail asking baby Doris for
money. Kidnapping threats were routine and the pampered "Million Dollar
Baby" was guarded from the public by a battery of nurses and bodyguards. Her
father showered her with toys, ponies, and expensive gifts but didn't allow many

friends to play with her in her gilded cage. He was obsessed with germs so he bought a private Pullman car (naming it *Doris*) to isolate her from the public on her travels between their New York mansion, their country farm estate in New Jersey, and their Newport, Rhode Island, beach house.

The richest girl in the world grew up in the rarified air of over-the-top extravagance where dinner guests at parties would be given unimaginable party favors. At one such Newport party, rubies, sapphires, emeralds, and diamonds were buried in sand at the center of the table, and the guests were given sterling silver shovels and pails to dig for their treasures.

Doris and her fellow "poor little rich girl" Barbara Hutton, heiress to the Woolworth fortune, became jaded young women in this atmosphere of excess and their competitive pursuit of excitement became legendary. The "gold dust twins," as they were known, were frequent guests on the party circuit and had lavish debutante balls of their own in the same year. As a result of their astronomical wealth "Dee Dee" and "Babs" developed different behavioral problems. While Barbara Hutton became the victim of her own excess, Doris Duke never learned the value of money and became known as one of the smallest tippers among the young social set. She often carried no cash on her, which meant others were stuck with the cab fare or the restaurant bill. Barbara squandered her money in grand gestures while Doris held back, burdened by the obligations of such a fortune.

In adulthood Doris Duke became fascinated with Hawaiians and their culture and, with her husband Jimmy Cromwell, she rented a cottage in Hawaii. She started taking hula lessons and spent her days on the beach at Waikiki. Doris found peace in the simple pleasures of island life and was frequently seen surfing. She befriended Olympic swimming champion Duke Kahanamoku, who was also the sheriff of Honolulu. She spent time swimming and surfing with Kahanamoku and eventually she was considered one of the best female surfers on the island. The Cromwells built a vacation house in Honolulu and Doris dubbed it Shangri-la. The heiress on her surfboard near her Diamond Head home is the inspiration for the following party.

Surf Party

Every surfer needs energy, and dates are packed with the source of it in the form of natural sugars. The Date Smoothie is a surfer's delight—just sip and go. Chocolate Chip Banana Bread takes advantage of the produce of Hawaii. Bananas and cocoa beans are both grown there and high quality chocolate is produced from the locally grown cocoa beans. Another Hawaiian crop is pineapple and it is put on a stick with tropical delights such as mangos, coconut, and bananas along with pound cake in Tropical Fruit Brochettes for a refreshing beach-worthy snack. Fish Tacos are the perfect beach party food, with a squeeze of lime that adds a splash of sunshine to your tongue. You can bring the flavors of the beach to your table with this menu even if it is cold and snowing outside. Just serve up the tacos on beach ball motif paper plates and the fruit brochettes in plastic sand pails. Place your "sidewalk surfboard" (skateboard) in a pile of sand in the center of the table, line it with banana leaves, and serve the banana bread slices on it. Decorate the edge of the table with hula skirts and hang loose!

Date Smoothie

SERVES 2

INGREDIENTS:

1 cup chopped dates

1 cup milk

1 banana

1 cup vanilla yogurt

¼ cup orange juice

4 scoops vanilla ice cream

METHOD:

1. Soak the dates in the milk for about an hour to soften them.

2. Purée the dates, milk, and banana in a blender.

3. Add the yogurt, orange juice, and ice cream and blend until smooth.

Chocolate Chip Banana Bread

Serves 6

INGREDIENTS:

¾ cup sugar

¼ cup honey

6 ounces unsalted soft butter

2 eggs, beaten

1 teaspoon vanilla

4 ripe bananas, mashed

2 cups flour

1½ teaspoons baking soda

½ teaspoon salt

½ cup chopped macadamia nuts

¼ cup shredded coconut

½ cup chocolate chips

METHOD:

1. Preheat oven to 350 degrees F. Grease a 9-inch x 5-inch loaf pan and set aside.

2. Combine sugar, honey, and butter in a mixing bowl and beat with an electric mixer until fluffy and light yellow in color.

continued

3. Add eggs and vanilla and mix well. Add bananas and mix well.

4. Combine flour, baking soda, and salt in a separate bowl and then add it to the batter, mixing well.

5. Fold in the macadamia nuts, coconut, and chocolate chips.

6. Scrape the batter into the prepared loaf pan and bake the bread for 1 hour and 10 minutes, or until a wooden skewer inserted in the middle comes out clean.

Tropical Fruit Brochettes

SERVES 6

INGREDIENTS:

½ cup shredded coconut

12 pound cake cubes, cut into one-inch squares

1 banana

12 strawberries

6 mango chunks

6 fresh pineapple chunks

6 bamboo skewers

Method:

1. Preheat oven to 350 degrees F.

2. Toast the coconut and the pound cake cubes in the oven for 10–15 minutes. Let cool.

3. Peel the banana and cut it into 6 chunks.

4. Thread one strawberry onto each skewer followed by a cube of pound cake, a banana chunk, a mango chunk, a pineapple chunk, another pound cake cube, and finish with a strawberry.

5. Sprinkle toasted coconut on the fruit.

Fish Tacos

Serves 6
Ingredients:

12 corn tortillas

½ cup diced tomato

¼ cup diced onion

1 tablespoon chopped cilantro

¼ cup diced avocado

1 tablespoon lemon juice

continued

1½ pounds firm white fish, such as
    halibut or snapper

½ cup cornmeal, seasoned with
    salt and pepper to taste

1 tablespoon olive oil

1 cup shredded purple cabbage

¼ cup tartar sauce

6 lime wedges

METHOD:

1. Warm the tortillas wrapped in paper towels in the microwave for
   15 seconds and then wrap them in foil to keep them warm.

2. In a bowl, combine the diced tomato, onion, cilantro, avocado, and
   lemon juice. Set aside.

3. Cut fish into strips, dredge them in the cornmeal mixture, and sear them
   in olive oil for about 5 minutes. Drain on paper towels.

4. Break the fish into bite-sized chunks. Fill the warm tortillas with the fish.

5. Top the fish with the shredded cabbage, then the tomato/avocado mixture.

6. Serve with tartar sauce and lime wedges.

New Year's Eve with The Thin Man

Nora Charles

Dashiell Hammett, former Pinkerton detective and author of *The Maltese Falcon*, created the characters of Nick and Nora Charles in his detective novel, *The Thin Man*. Nick is a retired private detective and Nora a wealthy socialite whose personality was allegedly modeled after Hammett's lover, playwright Lillian Hellman. Myrna Loy brings Nora Charles to life in the movie rendition of the story, starring opposite William Powell as Nick. The witty banter between the Charleses provides comic relief while the plot thickens. Intrigue and murder are interwoven with constant cocktails and a party scene hosted by the Charleses in their luxury hotel suite. With a festive backdrop of glittering holiday decorations and a shiny, silver Christmas tree, Nora graciously shakes her martinis and totes a tray of stemware around the suite, offering drinks to her guests. Her witty perception of situations led to her reputation that one could not pull a fast one over on the no-nonsense Mrs. Charles. Being clever in a graceful and politic manner and a blend of humor, style, and a touch of sarcasm were Nora's hallmarks. The following party is the way Nora would spend New Year's Eve.

A Sophisticated New Year's Eve Party

Plan a tasteful dinner party to ring in the New Year with style, and serve your guests an elegant meal of rich, decadent dishes. Encourage your guests to wear formal party attire, such as tuxedos and Art Deco gowns with bangles and bobbles adorning their ears, necks, and wrists. (These may be found at a vintage clothing store or costume shop at reasonable prices.) Provide party tiaras, hats, and noisemakers for your guests and have jazz music playing as they arrive. Start your sophisticated soiree with the simple and elegant Caviar Puffs and cocktails. After the cocktail hour call the guests to the dinner table for an appetizer of Cornmeal Blinis drizzled with clarified butter and surrounded with red grapes. Follow the opener with a luscious Brie Fondue served with dippers of shrimp, bread cubes, and blanched vegetables. Finish the meal with Chocolate Champagne Truffles and a glass of bubbly. The Cognac-flavored truffles are rolled in tan-colored raw sugar making them look like Champagne bubbles. Provide the entertainment of several *Thin Man* movies and spend the midnight hour and beyond with Nora Charles.

Caviar Puffs

SERVES 8

INGREDIENTS:

1 sheet frozen puff pastry, thawed

1 egg, beaten with 2 tablespoons water

½ cup sour cream

1 ounce black caviar

2 tablespoons chopped chives

METHOD:

1. Preheat oven to 400 degrees F.

2. Cut shapes, such as stars or flowers, out of the puff pastry sheet with a cookie cutter and put them on a parchment paper-lined cookie sheet.

3. Brush the pastry with the beaten egg mixture.

4. Bake the pastry for 15 minutes, turn the oven down to 325 degrees F, and bake for 10 minutes more.

5. Cool the pastry before garnishing.

6. Garnish each pastry with a teaspoon of sour cream, a ¼ teaspoon of caviar, and a sprinkle of chives.

Cornmeal Blinis

SERVES 8

INGREDIENTS:

1 cup cornmeal

½ teaspoon salt

1½ cups boiling water

2 eggs

1 cup milk

½ cup flour

2 tablespoons melted butter

¾ cup clarified butter

½ cup red grapes

½ cup sour cream

¼ cup fresh dill sprigs

freshly ground black pepper

METHOD:

1. In a bowl combine the cornmeal and salt, then stir in the boiling water. Cover and let stand for 10 minutes.

2. Beat in the eggs one at a time.

3. Stir in the milk, then the flour, and finally the melted butter. Beat until smooth.

4. Fry the blinis in the clarified butter on a griddle or crepe pan. Turn each over like a pancake and cook the other side.

5. Cut the grapes in half lengthwise.

6. Garnish the warm blinis with a drizzle of clarified butter, a dollop of sour cream, a dill sprig, black pepper, and the grape halves.

Brie Fondue

SERVES 8

INGREDIENTS:

1 minced shallot

1 tablespoon butter

6 ounces freshly squeezed pink grapefruit juice

6 ounces white wine

2 tablespoons flour

2 pounds Brie cheese

1 teaspoon pink grapefruit zest

2 tablespoons chives

½ teaspoon white pepper

1 loaf French bread

1 pound cooked shrimp, chilled

1 cup blanched asparagus tips

1 cup blanched baby carrots

bamboo skewers

METHOD:

1. Sauté the shallot in the butter until tender.

2. Deglaze the pan by adding the wine and grapefruit juice and reduce over medium heat to one cup.

3. While the wine and juice are reducing, cut the rind off the Brie and cut it into chunks. Toss the chunks with the flour.

4. To the reduced liquid, add the flour-coated Brie a little at a time and stir constantly to melt it. When all the cheese has been added and melted, remove from heat.

5. Stir in the grapefruit zest, pepper, and chives, and put the fondue in a fondue pot over a flame.

6. Cut the bread into cubes.

7. Serve the fondue with the skewers, bread cubes, shrimp, asparagus, and carrots surrounding it.

Chocolate Champagne Truffles

SERVES 8

INGREDIENTS:

8 ounces semisweet chocolate chips

8 ounces cream

2 ounces unsalted butter

1 ounce Cognac

5 ounces white chocolate chips

1 ounce salted butter

1 cup raw sugar

  foil candy cups

METHOD:

1. In a bowl combine the semisweet chocolate with 6 ounces of cream, 1 ounce of unsalted butter, and the Cognac.

2. In another bowl combine the white chocolate with 1 ounce of cream, 1 ounce of unsalted butter, and 1 ounce of salted butter.

3. Set both bowls over hot water to melt the chocolates and then stir the liquids into the chocolates until smooth and well mixed.

continued

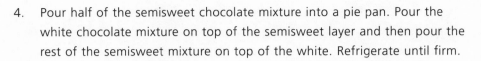

4. Pour half of the semisweet chocolate mixture into a pie pan. Pour the white chocolate mixture on top of the semisweet layer and then pour the rest of the semisweet mixture on top of the white. Refrigerate until firm.

5. Scoop out balls of the firm chocolate and put the truffle balls on a plastic lined tray. Roll balls between palms to make them more uniform.

6. Roll the truffles in the raw sugar and place them in foil candy cups. Refrigerate until ready to serve.

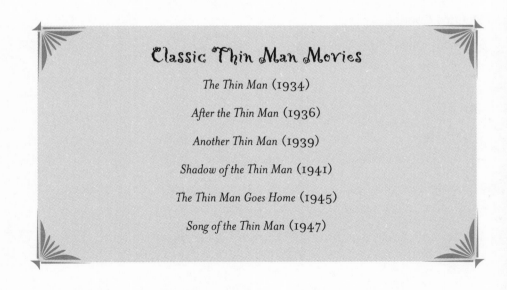

Classic Thin Man Movies

The Thin Man (1934)

After the Thin Man (1936)

Another Thin Man (1939)

Shadow of the Thin Man (1941)

The Thin Man Goes Home (1945)

Song of the Thin Man (1947)

Chapter 2

Hollywood Hostesses

Sophia Loren's Pajama Party

Sophia Loren

Actress Sophia Loren has appeared in over one hundred movies, including *Two Women* for which she won the first Best Actress Oscar in a foreign film. Born into poverty in Pozzuoli, Italy, she transformed overnight from a skinny girl to a voluptuous woman at age fourteen and won a beauty contest. Though her prize was not much more than a few rolls of wallpaper, she was encouraged to try her hand (and face and figure) at another contest to become Queen of the Sea. She only achieved princesshood but she caught the eye of producer Carlo Ponti who arranged for her first screen test. Screen tests would lead to acting roles and love. Ponti would become her husband, winning her amore over Cary Grant, who only got to play the role of her husband in *Houseboat*. The pairing of Sophia and frequent costar Marcello Mastroianni epitomized the modern Italian-film genre so much that his other leading ladies were often Sophia look-alikes. Leading lady Sophia shared the screen with many leading men besides Mastroianni, including Peter Sellers, John Wayne, Marlon Brando, Charlton Heston, Paul Newman, Peter O'Toole, Richard Burton, and Omar Sharif.

Sophia's love for cooking and food is evidenced in fiction and reality. She has authored a cookbook and gastronomic biography, *In the Kitchen with*

Love; has played a pizza girl in *The Gold of Naples*; and her real-life cooking was once featured on the cover of a London magazine (along with her famous cleavage). She once said "Everything you see I owe to spaghetti," and that magazine cover bears witness to the connection. The silver screen queen's quip attributing her bountiful beauty to the noodle inspired this "girls' night in" dedicated to Ms. Loren's comfort food. Get comfortable—spaghetti straps optional!

Pasta Pajama Party

Here are a few recipes to whip up for this party. The Neopolitan Ice Cream Cake is a nod to Sophia Loren's role as a pizza girl in Naples. Make your life easy and purchase prewashed salad greens, your favorite brand of sauces, and ready-to-bake garlic bread. You can purchase meatballs from a carry-out restaurant or deli. Heat the meatballs, sauté the mushrooms, grill the shrimp, heat the sauces, and cook the pasta before the girls arrive so you'll be free to dish with them while they dish up their own dinners. Start the evening with Italian opera in the background and a chilled Campari and soda or a glass of Chianti while you toss the salad. Ciao down!

Pasta Pajama Party Options

SAUCES:
Pesto
Alfredo
Marinara

PASTAS:
Penne
Fettuccini
Spaghetti

ACCOMPANIMENTS:
Mushrooms
Meatballs
Grilled Shrimp
Parmigiano-Reggiano Cheese
Green Salad
Garlic Bread
Balsamic Vinaigrette
Parmesan Crisps
Neapolitan Ice Cream Cake
with Biscotti Crust

Balsamic Vinaigrette

SERVES 8
INGREDIENTS:

1 garlic clove

1 teaspoon coarse salt

¼ teaspoon pepper

1 teaspoon Dijon mustard

3 tablespoons balsamic vinegar ½ cup extra virgin olive oil

2 tablespoons red wine vinegar salt and pepper to taste

METHOD:

1. Mash the garlic clove, salt, and pepper together with the back of a wooden spoon in a large wooden bowl to form a paste.

2. Mix in the Dijon mustard and then the balsamic and red wine vinegars.

3. Slowly drizzle the olive oil into the bowl while stirring with a whisk.

4. Adjust seasoning with salt and pepper.

5. Leave dressing in the bowl until it's time to serve, then add salad greens and toss to coat them with the dressing.

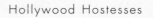

Classic Pesto

SERVES 8

INGREDIENTS:

4 cups packed fresh basil leaves

4 cloves peeled garlic

⅔ cup toasted pine nuts

1 cup olive oil

½ cup grated parmesan cheese

1 teaspoon salt

1 teaspoon plain yogurt

METHOD:

1. In a food processor, chop the garlic and pine nuts together to make a paste.

2. Add the basil and 2 tablespoons of the oil to the food processor and process with the nuts and garlic.

3. With the processor running and the pour hole on the top open, pour the rest of the oil in a thin stream into the basil mixture to form a purée.

4. Add the parmesan cheese and salt and process to blend.

5. Stir in the yogurt to help prevent the pesto from turning black.

Parmesan Lace Crisps

SERVES 8

INGREDIENTS:

½ cup grated Parmesan cheese

METHOD:

1. Preheat oven to 400 degrees F.

2. Place one tablespoon of Parmesan cheese for each crisp on a nonstick cookie sheet or a silicone baking sheet on a sheet pan. Space the crisps ½ inch apart.

3. With the back of the spoon, press down each tablespoon of cheese to flatten the mounds.

4. Bake for 3–5 minutes until golden and crisp.

5. Let the crisps cool and gently lift them off the cookie sheet.

6. Serve with salad as a garnish.

Neapolitan Ice Cream Cake with Biscotti Crust

SERVES 8

INGREDIENTS:

8 ounces biscotti cookies

3 ounces melted butter

2 tablespoons sugar

¼ cup pistachios, shelled

1 pint chocolate ice cream

1 pint strawberry ice cream

1 pint vanilla ice cream

METHOD:

1. Preheat oven to 350 degrees F.

2. Grind the biscotti in a food processor into crumbs.

3. Put the biscotti crumbs in a bowl with the melted butter, sugar, and pistachios and mix them together.

4. Press the biscotti crust mixture into the bottom of a springform pan and bake the crust for 15 minutes. Cool.

5. Soften the ice cream at room temperature for 5 minutes so it will spread easily.

6. Spread all of the chocolate ice cream over the cooled biscotti crust, creating a layer.

7. Spread the strawberry ice cream over the chocolate ice cream, creating another layer.

8. Spread the vanilla ice cream over the strawberry ice cream, creating the top layer.

9. Chill the ice cream cake for at least 1 hour so the layers can firm up.

10. To serve, remove the side ring of the springform pan and cut the cake into wedge-shaped slices.

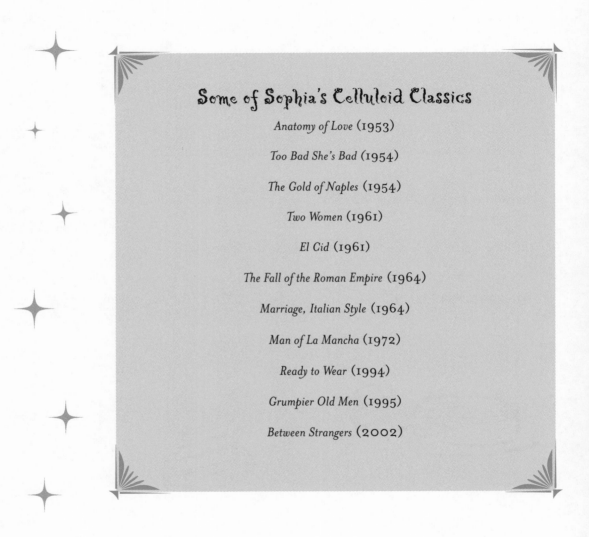

Some of Sophia's Celluloid Classics

Anatomy of Love (1953)

Too Bad She's Bad (1954)

The Gold of Naples (1954)

Two Women (1961)

El Cid (1961)

The Fall of the Roman Empire (1964)

Marriage, Italian Style (1964)

Man of La Mancha (1972)

Ready to Wear (1994)

Grumpier Old Men (1995)

Between Strangers (2002)

Mother's Day with Mommie Dearest

Joan Crawford

Lucille LeSueur was an MGM contract chorus girl who became Joan Crawford after a magazine contest was held in 1925 to rename her in order to make her more appealing to the public. As Lucille, she had danced the night away at the Cocoanut Grove in Los Angeles, frequently winning Charleston contests and garnering dozens of trophies as well as show business press coverage. F. Scott Fitzgerald thought of her as "doubtless the best example of the flapper: The girl you see in smart nightclubs; gowned to the apex of sophistication; toying iced glasses with a remote, faintly bitter expression; dancing deliciously; laughing a great deal with wide, hurt eyes; young things with a talent for living."

The first parts Joan played were showgirls dancing in silent films. She didn't take acting seriously until she observed Lon Chaney's intense devotion to the craft when she starred with him as a carney girl in *The Unknown* (1927). Unlike other actresses of the silent film era, Joan Crawford made the transition smoothly to talking pictures. Her roles moved on from chorus girl to shop girl as she portrayed the type of independent American woman who didn't need a man to take care of her. The Academy Award for Best Actress was given to her for *Mildred Pierce* in 1945. A few years later she portrayed a woman who was obsessed with cleanliness and cared more for her house than her family in *Harriet Craig*, mirroring what was going on in her real life. After that her movie roles started to become film noir in nature, eventually sliding down a slippery slope into the outright bizarre. She even filled in for her ill daughter on a soap opera in the 1960s, vainly playing a role meant for a woman much younger than she was. From flapper to shop girl to camp queen to pathetic soap star, Joan never wavered in her ambition.

The ugly side of Joan Crawford's personal life was exposed after her death, when her adopted daughter Christina, who had been cut from her will, wrote the book *Mommie Dearest*. "Mommie Dearest" had been a term of endearment the children were supposed to say to their mother, but it turned into a term of resentment as a result of the abuse Joan dished out. She terrorized her children with night raids, tearing their clothes off forbidden wire hangers and trashing the bathroom before forcing them to clean up the mess to spotless perfection. Joan Crawford was a woman of extremes. She exhibited a slavish devotion to her fans—personally autographing photographs, diligently answering fan mail, and making personal appearances at fan club luncheons; but sadly she fell far short of becoming mother of the year.

Mildred Pierce's Chicken Dinner

In honor of Joan Crawford's Oscar winning role as the housewife-turned-restaurateur Mildred Pierce, I offer you a chicken dinner like the one served at Mildred's. Mildred's daughter, Veda, complained of her mother's chicken and her pies but they made possible the glitzy lifestyle that the ungrateful

Veda was leading. (Ironically, the roles were reversed for the real life Mommie Dearest and her on-screen daughter dearest here.) Your daughter won't complain about the Roast Chicken with Deluxe Mashed Potatoes and Blueberry Pie when the aromas emerge from the kitchen; or perhaps she should be making this dinner for you on Mother's Day.

Two bonus recipes follow the chicken dinner. To commemorate the pairing of screen rivals Bette Davis and Joan Crawford in the movie classic *What Ever Happened to Baby Jane?*, there is a recipe for What Ever Happened to Baby Back Ribs. And in a nod to Joan's Pepsi days when she was married to the chairman of the board of Pepsi, there is a recipe for Cola Glazed Pork Chops. So if anyone complains like Veda did about the chicken, you have options.

Roast Chicken

SERVES 4

INGREDIENTS:

4-pound roasting chicken, rinsed and insides removed

1 teaspoon salt

1 teaspoon pepper

bunch of green onions

1 lemon, cut in half

1 orange, cut in quarters

continued

3 "coins" of fresh ginger root

1 tablespoon soft butter

1 leek, julienned

METHOD:

1. Preheat oven to 350 degrees F.

2. Season the inside of the chicken with half of the salt and pepper, and then tuck the wings under the front of the bird.

3. Stuff the chicken with the green onions, lemon, orange, and ginger root.

4. Rub the soft butter over the skin of the chicken, and then sprinkle it with the rest of the salt and pepper.

5. Place the leeks on the bottom of a roasting pan and put the chicken on top of them.

6. Roast the chicken uncovered until the legs wiggle easily and juices run clear when poked in the thigh, about 1½ hours.

7. Remove chicken from the oven and let it rest at least 15 minutes before carving.

Deluxe Mashed Potatoes

SERVES 4

INGREDIENTS:

1½ pounds potatoes, peeled
    and cubed

4 ounces cream cheese, softened

4 ounces butter, soft

¼ cup sour cream

¼ cup milk

1 egg, beaten

2 tablespoons minced onion

    salt and white pepper to taste

METHOD:

1. Preheat oven to 350 degrees F.

2. Put potatoes in cold salted water, bring to a boil, and cook for 15 minutes.

3. Drain potatoes and let sit for a minute to let some of the steam escape.

4. Beat the potatoes with an electric mixer until smooth.

5. Add cream cheese and beat again.

6. Add butter and beat until blended.

7. Mix in sour cream, then milk, eggs, onion, and seasoning. Put mixture into a buttered casserole dish. (At this point the dish can be refrigerated overnight if preparing ahead of time.)

8. Bake uncovered for 45 minutes until lightly browned.

Blueberry Pie

SERVES 8

INGREDIENTS:

2 rolled out circles of pie dough

5 cups blueberries

½ cup dried blueberries

1 cup plus 2 tablespoons sugar

½ teaspoon cinnamon

4 tablespoons cornstarch

¼ cup lemon juice

1 ounce butter, cut in pieces

1 tablespoon cream

METHOD:

1. Preheat oven to 350 degrees F. Line pie pan with one circle of pie dough.

2. Mix blueberries and dried blueberries together with 1 cup of sugar, cinnamon, lemon juice, and cornstarch and put them in the pie shell. Dot the blueberries with the butter pieces.

3. Cover the blueberry filling with the other pie dough circle, crimp the edges to seal, and cut slits in the top.

4. Brush the piecrust with the cream and sprinkle with 2 tablespoons of sugar. Bake for 50 minutes. Cool before slicing.

Cola Glazed Pork Chops

SERVES 4

INGREDIENTS:

4 pork chops, 1½ inches thick

4 slices sweet onion

1 cup cola

   salt and pepper to taste

METHOD:

1. Preheat oven to 350 degrees F.

2. Put pork chops in a baking dish and place one onion slice on top of each chop.

3. Pour the cola over the onions and pork chops, and then sprinkle them with salt and pepper.

4. Bake for 15 minutes, baste with the cola and juices in the pan, and bake for 10 minutes more.

What Ever Happened to Baby Back Ribs?

SERVES 4

INGREDIENTS:

¼ cup paprika

1 tablespoon chili powder

2 cloves minced garlic

4 teaspoons salt

2 teaspoons brown sugar

2 teaspoons pepper

2 teaspoons dried oregano

2 teaspoons dried thyme

2 slabs baby back pork ribs

2½ cups barbecue sauce

METHOD:

1. Preheat oven to 350 degrees F.

2. Mix spices together in a bowl and then rub all of the mixture on both sides of the ribs. Refrigerate for up to 24 hours.

3. Place ribs in a roasting pan, cover with foil, and bake for 2 hours. Remove from the oven and uncover the ribs. These can be refrigerated now and grilled later if you are preparing ahead of time.

4. Preheat a grill when it is time to serve the ribs. (If you don't have a grill you can cook them in the oven uncovered following the same directions.)

5. Brush ½ cup of the barbecue sauce on the ribs and grill for 5 minutes. Turn ribs over and brush another ½ cup of the sauce on them and grill for 5 minutes. Turn ribs over one more time and brush with another ½ cup of sauce and grill another 5 minutes.

6. Cut the slabs into individual ribs and pile on a platter.

7. Heat the remaining cup of barbecue sauce and serve it on the side with the ribs.

From Pretty Lady to Troglodyte

Joan Crawford's last film was *Trog* in 1970. In this sci-fi horror movie, she plays an anthropologist who befriends and tries to train the "missing link" to coexist with humans. Her Technicolor image is a caricature of herself. It is a macabre ending to an illustrious movie career that started in 1925 with a role as a carefree chorus girl in *Pretty Ladies*.

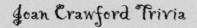

Joan Crawford Trivia

- Was once married to Douglas Fairbanks Jr., making her Mary Pickford's daughter-in-law.
- Became the Pepsi "Queen" after marrying the Pepsi-Cola chairman of the board, Alfred Steele, in 1955.
- Accepted the Best Actress Oscar for Mildred Pierce from her bed.
- Lived in the back room of a laundry as a child and had to help her mother by putting the clothes on wire hangers.

Famous Quotes

- "If you want to see the girl next door, go next door."
- "I need sex for a good complexion but I'd rather do it for love."
- "Not that anyone cares, but there's a right and wrong way to clean a house."
- Famous last words to her housekeeper who was praying for her on her deathbed: "Damn it! Don't you dare ask God to help me."

Must-See Joan Crawford Films

Pretty Ladies (1925)

Our Dancing Daughters (1928)

Grand Hotel (1932)

Letty Lynton (1932)

Rain (1932)

I Live My Life (1935)

The Women (1939)

Mildred Pierce (1945)

Possessed (1947)

Flamingo Road (1949)

Harriet Craig (1950)

The Damned Don't Cry (1950)

Queen Bee (1955)

What Ever Happened to Baby Jane? (1962)

Berserk! (1968)

Trog (1970)

Hollywood's Golden Girl at Pickfair

Mary Pickford

Silent film star Mary Pickford was once known as America's sweetheart: the first movie star and the most powerful woman in Hollywood. She invented acting for film, using more subtle gestures than stage acting, courting a close relationship with the camera which ended up conveying more emotion than the exaggerated formula in practice at the time. Her film career would not survive 'talkies' and she would retire at age forty-one with a legacy of 193 films. She was the first superstar created by film and the first "has been" created by the same medium.

Before she was America's sweetheart Mary Pickford was Gladys Smith, born in Toronto, Canada, in 1892. She made her stage debut in a Victorian melodrama called *The Silver King* at age seven for eight dollars a week. In New York in 1907, a fifteen-year-old Gladys made her Broadway debut as a David Belasco player with the stage name of Mary Pickford, earning a salary of twenty-five dollars a week. When the show folded her mother encouraged her to seek a job in the new moving pictures industry, which Mary considered a step down from stage acting, but her fatherless family needed money desperately so she complied. She was hired by D.W. Griffith at Biograph Studios for one hundred dollars a week and her film career began. In 1913, after scores of short films for Biograph, Mary signed with Adolph Zukor's company, Famous Players, at five hundred dollars a week. At age twenty-one, Mary Pickford was the highest paid actress in the world.

She was a celebrity of unparalleled popularity, thanks to motion picture fan magazines such as *Photoplay*. She played the roles of darling young girls and feisty, independent heroines in a way that challenged the established norm of how females should behave. Superstardom came with her roles in the new, longer feature films *Tess of the Storm Country* and *Rags*. She negotiated the renewal of her contract with Zukor, and his distribution company Paramount Pictures, in 1916 for a salary of ten thousand dollars a week. Talk about rags to riches!

In 1919, Mary Pickford, Douglas Fairbanks, Charlie Chaplin, and D.W. Griffith formed United Artists, a production company to produce and distribute their own films. The film industry had moved to California by this time, and the following year, Mary and Douglas Fairbanks married and ascended to the throne of Hollywood royalty. Douglas's wedding gift to Mary was an eighteen-acre Beverly Hills estate that the press dubbed Pickfair. An invitation to Pickfair was highly coveted by everyone, from Amelia Earhart to Albert Einstein. You had "arrived" in Hollywood if you were invited to Pickfair.

Pickfair Picnic

You don't need to wait any longer for your invitation. You can invite your friends over to your "estate" and watch Mary Pickford movies before you pack a picnic basket with the following dishes and retire to the lawn. Mary Pickford and Douglas Fairbanks starred in a movie version of *The Taming of the Shrew*, in which Douglas's character Petruchio says, "Oh come Kate, come. You must not look so sour." And Mary's character Katherine responds, "It is my fashion when I see a crab." That prompted me to add crabmeat to the standard picnic fare of deviled eggs in Crabby Deviled Eggs. Potato salad is also a picnic staple but this one is given a twist by using sweet potatoes in honor of America's sweetheart in Sweet Potato Salad. Rounding out the picnic are finger sandwiches and cookies. The visually attractive and easy to serve Picnic Wraps are filled with cream cheese, salami, cheddar cheese and cucumbers, and the delicious Oatmeal Butterscotch Cookies are studded with butterscotch chips and golden raisins. This picnic is easy to pack, but not easy to forget. That's entertainment—Pickfair style.

Crabby Deviled Eggs

SERVES 6

INGREDIENTS:

6 eggs

¼ cup mayonnaise

1 teaspoon yellow mustard

1 tablespoon sour cream

2 tablespoons softened cream cheese

1 teaspoon salt

½ teaspoon pepper

¼ teaspoon cayenne pepper sauce

¼ cup crabmeat

2 tablespoons chopped fresh dill

METHOD:

1. Put the eggs in a saucepan and cover them with water. Bring water to a boil, turn to simmer and set the timer for 15 minutes. When done, pour out the hot water and replace with cold water. Change water several times until it is no longer warm. Drain and peel the shells off.

2. Cut the peeled eggs in half lengthwise, carefully remove the yolks, and set aside the white halves. Put the yolks in a bowl and mash with a fork.

3. Add mayonnaise, mustard, sour cream, and cream cheese to yolk mixture and mix together with a fork to a smooth paste.

4. Season the yolk mixture with salt, pepper, and cayenne pepper sauce.

5. Fill each egg white with a teaspoon of crabmeat.

6. Scoop about 1 tablespoon of the yolk filling into each white, covering the crabmeat so it is a hidden surprise.

7. Garnish the yolk filling with a sprinkle of chopped dill.

8. Cover and refrigerate until chilled.

Sweet Potato Salad

Ingredients:

2 pounds sweet potatoes

1½ cups mayonnaise

2 teaspoons Dijon mustard

¼ teaspoon salt

   pepper to taste

2 chopped hard-boiled eggs

1 cup diced celery

6 sliced green onions

Method:

1. Peel and dice the sweet potatoes.

2. Boil the diced sweet potatoes in salted water for 20 minutes, or until they are tender and can be pierced easily with the tip of a paring knife. Drain and cool.

3. In a bowl, mix the mayonnaise, mustard, salt, and pepper.

4. Add the cooled sweet potatoes, hard-boiled eggs, celery, and green onions to the mayonnaise mixture and toss gently to coat.

5. Cover and chill in the refrigerator 2 hours before serving.

Picnic Wraps

SERVES 6

INGREDIENTS:

1 cucumber, peeled and seeded

4 ounces cheddar cheese

4 ounces salami (whole, not sliced)

4 large (burrito size) flour tortillas

8 ounces whipped cream cheese

METHOD:

1. Cut the cucumber into julienne strips and set aside.

2. Cut the cheddar cheese into 4 long sticks and set aside.

3. Peel the paper off the salami and cut it into 4 long sticks and set aside.

continued

4. Lay the tortillas flat and divide the cream cheese evenly among them. Spread the cream cheese over the surface of the tortillas.

5. At the bottom of each tortilla place 1 cheddar stick, 1 salami stick, and 3 julienne strips of cucumber.

6. Roll each tortilla up around the filling from bottom to top to form 4 logs.

7. Cut the ends off each log then slice each log into 6 pieces.

8. Arrange the pieces on a platter with the cross-section facing up so the pattern of the filling is visible. Cover and chill until ready to serve.

Oatmeal Butterscotch Cookies

SERVES 6

INGREDIENTS:

3 ounces butter, softened

⅓ cup brown sugar

¼ cup sugar

1 egg

½ teaspoon vanilla

½ cup flour

1½ cups rolled oats

½ teaspoon salt

¼ teaspoon baking soda

¾ cup butterscotch chips

¾ cup golden raisins

METHOD:

1. Preheat oven to 350 degrees F.

2. With and electric mixer cream together the butter, brown sugar, and sugar until fluffy.

3. Add the egg and vanilla and combine well. Scrape down the bowl frequently during mixing.

4. Mix the oats, flour, salt and baking soda together in a bowl then add it to the butter mixture, stirring well to combine into a smooth dough.

5. Stir in the butterscotch chips and raisins.

6. Drop the dough into mounds, using an ice cream scoop or two spoons, onto a parchment-lined cookie sheet. Press down the mounds to flatten them slightly with a wet palm.

7. Bake for 12–15 minutes. Cool on a rack.

Sound Bite

"Adding sound to movies would be like putting lipstick on the
Venus de Milo." — MARY PICKFORD

Hair Matters

"You would have thought I murdered someone and perhaps I had,
but only to give her successor a chance to live."
— MARY PICKFORD *responding to the public's reaction to*
bobbing her trademark curls in 1928

The Golden Age

"We were pioneers in a brand new medium of art. Let no one tell you
that they don't miss their career. I miss it terribly. My pictures were
my whole life." — MARY PICKFORD

And The Oscar Goes To . . .

Mary Pickford and Douglas Fairbanks helped found the
Academy of Motion Picture Arts and Sciences in 1927.

A Cosmopolitan Happy Hour

Sex and the City

Sex and the City, the popular HBO cable television series about four Cosmopolitan-drinking New York girlfriends and their sex lives, became a phenomenon in the last years of the millennium and into Y2K, and the fascination continues now in syndication. The show is seen from the point of view of the character Carrie Bradshaw, who writes a newspaper column on the status of her contemporaries' sex lives. Because the show originally aired on HBO, many premium-cable-challenged people (myself included) didn't see it as it unfolded. We latecomers to the party are able to catch up on the details now since it is available to rent or buy on DVD and it is also being aired on TBS. What I did catch from the original buzz about the show was that it honestly, and with humor and philosophical undertones, portrayed the reality of the modern single thirty-something girl living in the Big City and trying to find happiness, satisfaction, and love—all with a glossy veneer of high fashion. The main characters of the show, played by actresses Sarah Jessica Parker, Kim Cattrall, Kristin Davis, and Cynthia Nixon, dated and often dumped or got dumped by characters played by actors Chris Noth, Kyle MacLachlan, John Corbett, Jon Bon Jovi, and Mikhail Baryshnikov, among others, while maneuvering through daily urban life and meeting in restaurants and cafes to discuss their affairs.

The women of *Sex and the City* haunt the happy hours of the city, sipping Cosmopolitans and gossiping on a regular basis. A deconstruction of the Cosmopolitan, which is a vodka cocktail containing cranberry juice and a squeeze of lime, is the basis for two of the following recipes for your own Happy Hour Party. Cranberry Turkey Endive Petals and Lime Bay Scallop Endive Petals are hip finger foods with splashy colors and contemporary flavors to liven up your hors d'oeuvres table. BLT Cups are an upscale version of the comfort food sandwich, without the bread, and Chocolate-Dipped Figs are an aphrodisiac perfect for this theme. Serve a buffet of these treats and a pitcher of Cosmopolitans, virgin or otherwise, and queue up your favorite episodes of *Sex and the City* for a stylishly comfortable party with friends.

Cranberry Turkey Endive Petals

SERVES 12

INGREDIENTS:

4 heads green endive lettuce

2 cups diced smoked turkey

½ cup dried cranberries

¼ cup diced celery

½ cup mayonnaise

salt and pepper to taste

½ cup toasted walnuts, chopped

METHOD:

1. Separate the endive leaves into individual petals and lay them out on a tray.

2. In a bowl, combine the smoked turkey, dried cranberries, celery, and mayonnaise and mix well. Season to taste with salt and pepper.

3. Put a tablespoon of the turkey salad on the bottom end of each endive petal.

4. Garnish each petal with a sprinkle of chopped walnuts.

5. Arrange the filled endive petals on a serving platter.

Lime Bay Scallop Endive Petals

SERVES 12

INGREDIENTS:

4 heads red endive lettuce

2 cups cooked bay scallops, steamed and chilled

¼ cup fresh lime juice

1 teaspoon grated lime zest

½ cup mayonnaise

1 tablespoon finely diced red bell pepper

METHOD:

1. Separate the endive into individual leaves and lay them out on a tray.

2. Toss the bay scallops in a bowl with the lime juice and set aside.

3. Combine the mayonnaise with the lime zest.

4. Put ½ teaspoon of the lime zest mayonnaise on the bottom end of each endive petal.

5. Drain the lime juice from the bay scallops and put 2-3 of them on top of the lime mayonnaise.

6. Garnish the scallops with a pinch of the red bell pepper.

BLT Cups

SERVES 12

INGREDIENTS:

36 cherry tomatoes

5 slices bacon

6 butter lettuce leaves

½ cup mayonnaise

METHOD:

1. Cut the top ¼ inch off of each cherry tomato.

2. Scoop the seeds and juice out of the cherry tomatoes with a demitasse spoon and set them upside down on several layers of paper towels to drain for 15 minutes.

3. Dice the bacon and fry it to make crisp bacon bits. Drain the grease and let the bacon bits cool.

4. Tear the lettuce leaves into bite-size pieces.

5. Put the mayonnaise in a squeeze bottle or piping bag.

6. Cut a small bit of the skin off at the bottom of each tomato to help them stand up and not roll around. Turn the tomato cups upright.

7. Squirt a dab of mayonnaise into each tomato.

8. Stick a piece of lettuce in each tomato so it is anchored in the mayonnaise and sticks out the top.

9. Place a few bacon bits on top of the mayonnaise in each tomato.

10. Serve on a lettuce-lined platter.

Chocolate-Dipped Figs

SERVES 12

INGREDIENTS:

8 ounces bittersweet chocolate, chopped

2 tablespoons cream

1 cup toasted hazelnuts

12 dried Calimyrna figs

12 fresh Black Mission figs

24 fluted paper candy cups (optional)

METHOD:

1. Put the cream and chocolate together in a bowl and set over hot water. When melted, stir to combine and remove from heat.

2. Finely chop the toasted hazelnuts and spread them out on a plate.

3. Dip each fig into the melted chocolate, covering the bottom third.

4. Dip the bottom of the chocolate-dipped fig into the chopped nuts and then set them on a tray covered with foil. Refrigerate until the chocolate sets.

5. Remove the figs from the refrigerator, peel them from the foil, and put them in the candy cups, if using.

6. Arrange the figs on several small plates to serve as petits fours.

Trivia

Sex and the City won eight Golden Globe Awards.
The final word of the very last episode is "Fabulous."

Quotes from Carrie Bradshaw

• "Hi, I'd like a cheeseburger, please, a large fries, and a Cosmopolitan."

• "So what are we going to do? Sit around bars, sipping Cosmos, and sleeping with strangers when we're eighty?"

• "Here. Swear. Swear on Chanel."

• "Maybe the past is like an anchor holding us back. Maybe you have to let go of who you were to become who you will be."

A Star is Born—Oscar

Queens of the Silver Screen

Since its formation in 1927, the Academy of Motion Picture Arts and Sciences has held an annual awards ceremony to recognize outstanding film achievement and encourage higher levels of quality in motion picture production. One of the categories has been for an actress in a leading role, AKA Best Actress. The winners receive a gold trophy of a knight gripping a sword standing on a reel of film. Officially named the Academy Award of Merit, the coveted golden statuette was nicknamed Oscar when Margaret Herrick, an Academy librarian at the time, said it resembled her Uncle Oscar. A Hollywood columnist referred to it as an Oscar in 1934 but the Academy didn't officially adopt the nickname until 1939.

The first Oscar for Best Actress was presented to Janet Gaynor at a private dinner banquet hosted by Academy President Douglas Fairbanks in the Blossom Room of the Hollywood Roosevelt Hotel in 1929. The first Best Supporting Actress award was presented in 1936 to Gale Sondergaard at the Biltmore Bowl of the Biltmore Hotel in Los Angeles. Over the years, award categories have been added and the venue for the presentation has moved to larger arenas, including The Cocoanut Grove of the Ambassador Hotel, Grauman's Chinese Theatre, the Shrine Civic Auditorium, the Academy Award Theatre, RKO Pantages Theatre, Santa Monica Civic Auditorium,

Dorothy Chandler Pavilion, and ultimately to the Kodak Theatre located across the street from where the original Oscars were awarded. Hosts, hostesses, and MCs of the annual event have included Bob Hope, Jack Benny, Fred Astaire, Danny Kaye, Donald O'Connor, Jerry Lewis, Frank Sinatra, Helen Hayes, Carol Burnett, Diana Ross, Shirley MacLaine, Goldie Hawn, Jane Fonda, Johnny Carson, Liza Minnelli, Chevy Chase, Billy Crystal, Whoopi Goldberg, David Letterman, Steve Martin, Chris Rock, and Jon Stewart.

Though even a nomination is an honor, a win is an achievement that puts an actress on the Mount Olympus of movie stardom. In the Silver Screen Queens' hierarchy there are actresses that have won two Oscars, including Betty Davis, Olivia de Havilland, Sally Field, Jane Fonda, Jodie Foster, Helen Hayes, Glenda Jackson, Jessica Lange, Vivien Leigh, Luise Rainer, Maggie Smith, Meryl Streep, Hilary Swank, Elizabeth Taylor, Dianne Wiest, and Shelley Winters. Ingrid Bergman has won three Oscars and Katherine Hepburn has won four, all for Best Actress. One of those four was a tie in 1968 with Barbra Streisand. Oscar "firsts" for Best Actresses include Mary Pickford for the first talking picture performance to win the award, Sophia Loren for the first foreign language performance, and Halle Berry as the first African-American woman to receive the award. Judy Garland was awarded a special Oscar in the form of a miniature statuette for her outstanding performance as a screen juvenile in *The Wizard of Oz*.

Oscar Party

The presentation of the Oscars over the years has blossomed from a small dinner party to a star-studded spectacle with multiple after-parties taking place all over Hollywood. In the first version of the movie A *Star is Born*, a scene depicts an early Oscar banquet. Ironically, the actress playing the role of the actress who wins the Oscar is Janet Gaynor, the first real Best Actress winner. Two remakes of the movie were done with Oscar winners Judy Garland and Barbra Streisand both playing the role. Ironically, none of those performances won the real Best Actress award!

When the Academy Awards roll around every spring you can host your own Oscar party, whether it's an intimate affair like the first banquet was or an extravaganza like the contemporary ceremonies are, with the following recipes. In honor of the state where the Oscars take place, there are Faux California Rolls, which are sushi-like wraps. Crepes Oscar get their name from a traditional culinary garnish that includes crabmeat, asparagus, and hollandaise sauce. The Cobb Salad was invented in the legendary Tinseltown movie star hangout, the Brown Derby restaurant. A decadent finish befitting the occasion is a Chocolate-Dipped Strawberry Cheesecake Tart that will finish your guests off just in time for popping the Champagne. The envelope please . . .

Faux California Rolls

SERVES 6

INGREDIENTS:

1 cucumber, peeled and seeded

2 avocados

4 large (burrito size) spinach
   flour tortillas

8 ounces whipped cream cheese

1 teaspoon wasabi paste

8 ounces imitation crab leg sticks

METHOD:

1. Cut the cucumber into long julienne strips, set aside.

2. Cut the avocados in half and remove the pits. Scoop out the avocado
   flesh with a large spoon; keep the halves intact and discard the skin. Cut
   each avocado half into 4 lengthwise slices, set aside.

3. Lay the tortillas flat and divide the cream cheese evenly among them.
   Spread the cream cheese over the surface of the tortillas.

4. Put a dab of wasabi paste on the cream cheese and spread it around.

continued

5. At the bottom of each tortilla place 2 crab leg sticks end to end, 4 avocado slices and 2 julienne strips of cucumber. Make sure the filling stretches completely from side to side.

6. Roll each tortilla up around the filling from bottom to top to form 4 logs.

7. Cut the ends off each log and then slice each log into 6 pieces.

8. Arrange the pieces on a platter with the cross-section facing up so the pattern of the filling is visible. Cover and chill until ready to serve.

9. Make these the day of the party because the avocado will turn brown if prepared too far in advance.

Crepes Oscar

SERVES 6

INGREDIENTS:

18 asparagus spears

5 lemon slices

1 cup crabmeat

18 crepes

¾ cup Hollandaise Sauce, warm

METHOD:

1. Snap one of the asparagus spears off at the bottom to see where the natural break is and then use it as a guide to cut the others.

2. Steam the asparagus until tender and then set aside to cool enough to handle.

3. Cut the lemon slices into quarters and set aside.

4. Drain any liquid from the crabmeat and pick out any shells or cartilage that may be left behind.

5. Roll up one steamed asparagus spear in each crepe and arrange the filled crepes in one layer in a baking dish.

6. Preheat the broiler.

7. Scatter the crabmeat in a line across the middle of each crepe.

8. Pour the hollandaise sauce over the crabmeat.

9. Place the baking dish under the broiler for a minute to brown.

10. Garnish each crepe with a lemon slice.

Cobb Salad

INGREDIENTS:

1 head iceberg lettuce, chopped

¾ cup Balsamic vinaigrette salad dressing (see recipe page 46)

2 tomatoes, diced

½ cup diced cooked chicken

1 avocado, diced

½ cup crumbled blue cheese

¼ cup bacon bits

3 chopped hard-boiled eggs

½ cup chopped green onions

METHOD:

1. Toss the lettuce leaves with the salad dressing.

2. Mound the dressed lettuce on an oval platter.

3. Arrange the remaining ingredients in individual stripes on top of the dressed lettuce.

Chocolate-Dipped Strawberry Cheesecake Tart

SERVES 6

INGREDIENTS:

2 cups finely chopped almonds

⅔ cup sugar

2 tablespoons flour

½ teaspoon salt

¼ cup melted butter

6 ounces cream cheese, softened

1½ teaspoons cornstarch

1 egg

¼ cup sour cream

1 teaspoon vanilla

18 strawberries

8 ounces semisweet chocolate, melted

METHOD:

1. Preheat oven to 350 degrees F.

2. Combine almonds, ⅓ cup sugar, flour, salt, and melted butter in a bowl.

3. Press the almond mixture into the bottom and sides of a greased 9½-inch fluted tart pan with a removable bottom. Set the tart pan on a baking sheet and bake for 15 minutes. Set aside while making filling.

continued

4. With an electric mixer beat the cream cheese until fluffy. Add ⅓ cup sugar and the cornstarch and cream together. Beat in the egg, scraping down the sides of the bowl, and then mix in the sour cream. Stir in the vanilla.

5. Pour this batter into the almond crust and bake for 20 minutes. Remove from oven and cool at room temperature and then chill completely in the refrigerator.

6. Dip the strawberries in the melted chocolate and set them on foil. Put them in the refrigerator to set.

7. Remove the outer ring from the tart pan and then place the chocolate-dipped strawberries on top of the tart.

Judy Garland

An Oscar was awarded for the song "Over the Rainbow,"
which was performed by Judy Garland in *The Wizard of Oz* (1939).
The T-oran-ato is in honor of the twister in that movie.

T-oran-ato: Tomato-Orange Tornado

SERVES 1

INGREDIENTS:

⅓ cup tomato juice

⅔ cup fresh-squeezed orange juice

   pinch celery salt

   dash Worcestershire sauce

¼ teaspoon horseradish

dash cayenne pepper sauce

1 shot vodka (optional)

METHOD:

1. Mix together the tomato juice, celery salt, Worcestershire sauce, horseradish, cayenne pepper sauce, and vodka (if using).

2. Pour the orange juice into a clear glass.

3. Pour the tomato juice mixture into the orange juice but don't stir it.

4. Swirl and drink!

Chapter 3

Literary Ladies

A Prizewinning Poetry Reading

Edna St. Vincent Millay

A baby girl born in 1892 named Edna St. Vincent Millay was destined to break out of the small town in Maine where she grew up to become the first woman to win the Pulitzer Prize for poetry. The future celebrated "girl poet" was given the unusual middle name of St. Vincent, after the hospital in New York that had nursed her Uncle Charlie (her mother's brother) back to health following a seafaring accident that nearly claimed his life. Charlie became a minor celebrity after the near fatal episode and went on the lecture circuit telling his tale of entrapment as a stowaway, his subsequent near-death experience, and the accompanying delirium that was followed by a miraculous rebirth. As in epic poetry, Edna's future was foreshadowed by her uncle's fame, but she would surpass his notoriety by quantum leaps and bounds.

As a child, Edna, or Vincent, as she was called, subscribed to a children's magazine, *St. Nicholas*, that held writing contests for budding young poets and awarded the winners with prizes and publication of their work. Vincent's first intentional writing of poetry began at age twelve when she received an honorable mention for her submission to *St. Nicholas*. At age fourteen she won the Gold Medal for her poem "The Land of Romance," which was reprinted in April 1907 by another publication, *Current Literature*. Early success was a confidence booster, but disappointment was not far behind. Edna St. Vincent Millay was not elected class poet of her senior class in high school. She was nominated by the girls, but the boys, who were constantly mocking her (mostly out of jealousy), nominated one of their own and she withdrew her nomination after their stamping and catcalling put an end to her attempts to deliver her acceptance speech.

In 1912, a poetry contest was advertised in a magazine stating that one hundred American poems would be published by *New York* publisher Mitchell Kennerly in a single volume called *The Lyric Yea*. Vincent wrote a poem, "Renascence," and submitted it hoping for the prize of one thousand dollars, which was to be awarded for the top three poems. While waiting for the results of the contest, Vincent went to a party with her sister Norma, where she ended up reciting "Renascence" to a spellbound audience. One of the party guests was so impressed with Vincent and her poem that she arranged for her colleagues to sponsor Vincent to attend Vassar College. Later that year "Renascence" was printed in *The Lyric Year*, but it was not awarded one of the top three prizes, resulting in cries from the literary community, including critics and fellow poets, that it should have received first prize. "Renascence" garnered recognition for Vincent that catapulted her into a larger world and changed the course of her life.

Edna St. Vincent Millay graduated from Vassar College in 1917. In 1918, her poem "First Fig" was published and Nancy Milford says in her biography of Vincent, *Savage Beauty: The Life of Edna St. Vincent Millay*, "Her cheeky quatrain ignited the imagination of a generation of American women: she gave them their rallying cry. A wild freedom edged with death." Milford goes on to say, "Edna St. Vincent Millay became the herald of the New Woman. She smoked in public when it was against the law for women to do so, she lived in Greenwich Village during the halcyon days of that starry bohemia, she slept with men and women and wrote about it in lyrics and sonnets that blazed with wit and a sexual daring that captivated the nation." In 1923, Vincent became the first woman to win the Pulitzer Prize for poetry. She published many volumes of her poems, even selling 35,000 copies of a collection of her sonnets within the first few weeks of its publication in the midst of the Great Depression. She drew sold-out crowds from coast to coast for her poetry readings, filling lecture halls with audiences clamoring to see the passionate and charming performance of the muse come to life.

Wine and Cheese Tasting

A wine and cheese tasting is an appropriate way to serve food at a poetry reading, creating a Bohemian atmosphere with the food and drink combination favored by artists through the ages. Guests are able to sample and savor at their own pace as they listen to the poem recitations of their fellow partygoers. The poetry selections can be a combination of originals, classics, and favorites of yours and your guests. Provide the participants with a stage area and set the spread of food and wines out in the back and around the perimeter of the space, leaving room for seating in the front and center. A living room, library, or den are all cozy spaces to house the event, or a corner in a local café or bookstore, if you can arrange it, would be an authentic setting. Be sure to label the wines and cheeses for your guests so they don't need to disrupt the entertainment to find out what they are eating and drinking. One red wine, perhaps a Merlot, and one white wine, such as Chardonnay, are sufficient to go with any of these recipes, so don't worry about buying lots of different wines if you want to keep the drinks simple. In addition to the wine, make available for your guests at least one nonalcoholic beverage, such as iced tea, ginger ale, or mineral water. The following recipes employ a variety of different cheeses and all are wine friendly. Gruyère Gougères, which are simply elegant cheese puffs, are a traditional accompaniment for wine tasting in France as a palate cleanser between sips. To make Brie Wellington, follow the recipe to wrap a whole wheel of baby Brie in puff pastry, the same way beef Wellington is made. Parmesan Cheddar Dates are a sweet and savory cookie-cracker and Cambozola Truffles are creamy, blue cheese tinged mouth-fuls that resemble the prized rhizome for which they are named. Budding Sapphos will be honored by an invitation to share their poems at a reception such as this.

Gruyère Gougères

SERVES 6

INGREDIENTS:

1 cup water

4 ounces unsalted butter

½ teaspoon salt

1 cup flour

4 eggs

1½ cups grated Gruyere cheese

METHOD:

1. Preheat oven to 400 degrees F. Line a cookie sheet with parchment paper.

2. Put the water, butter, and salt in a saucepan over medium high heat and bring to a boil. When butter is melted turn heat to medium and add the flour all at once. Stir constantly with a wooden spoon over medium heat until it is the consistency of mashed potatoes.

3. Remove from heat and put the flour mixture into a mixing bowl. Beat in the eggs one at a time with an electric mixer. Stir in 1 cup of the Gruyère cheese.

4. Scoop the dough with a small ice cream scoop or two spoons onto the prepared cookie sheet, evenly spacing them about 2 inches apart. Sprinkle them with the remaining cheese.

5. Bake 15 minutes, reduce heat to 350 degrees, and bake 15 minutes more. Serve warm or at room temperature.

Brie Wellington

SERVES 6

INGREDIENTS:

1 baby Brie wheel

2 tablespoons dried cherries

2 tablespoons sliced toasted almonds

1 tablespoon brown sugar

1 sheet frozen puff pastry, thawed

1 egg, beaten

butchers twine

METHOD:

1. Preheat oven to 400 degrees F.

2. Cut the wheel of Brie in half horizontally using unflavored dental floss, and separate the top from the bottom.

3. Arrange the dried cherries and almonds on the bottom half of the Brie and sprinkle them with the brown sugar.

4. Place the top of the Brie on top of the filling and gently press down.

5. Unfold the puff pastry on a floured surface and roll it out so it is big enough to enclose the whole wheel of Brie.

6. Place the Brie in the middle of the puff pastry and draw the sides up and around, gathering it at the top like a pouch. Tie a piece of butcher's twine around the top to close the pouch.

7. Brush the beaten egg on the pastry.

8. Bake the pastry-encased Brie on a baking sheet lined with parchment paper for 20 minutes, reduce the heat to 325 degrees F, and bake another 20 minutes.

9. Remove the butchers twine and serve warm.

Parmesan Cheddar Dates

SERVES 8

INGREDIENTS:

2 ounces unsalted butter, softened

1 tablespoon grated Parmesan cheese

2 ounces sharp cheddar cheese, shredded

⅛ teaspoon salt

½ cup flour

pinch ground cayenne pepper

16 whole pitted dates

¼ cup slivered almonds

¼ cup melted butter

METHOD:

1. Preheat oven to 350 degrees F.

2. Cream the butter, cheeses, salt, and cayenne pepper together with an electric mixer.

3. Add the flour and combine to form a dough.

4. Roll the dough into a 1-inch diameter log and refrigerate while preparing the dates.

continued

5. Cut the dates in half lengthwise, and stuff each date half with a slivered almond.

6. Cut the dough log into ¼-inch slices and press an almond-stuffed date onto each slice, almond side up.

7. Put the slices on a baking sheet and brush them with melted butter.

8. Bake 10 minutes. Serve warm or at room temperature.

Cambozola Truffles

SERVES 8

INGREDIENTS:

6 ounces Cambozola cheese

2 ounces unsalted butter, softened

2 ounces cream cheese, softened

1 ounce Cognac

salt and white pepper to taste

2 cups fresh pumpernickel bread crumbs

Method:

1. Beat the Cambozola, butter, cream cheese, and Cognac together until smooth. Season with salt and pepper and then refrigerate for 4 hours or up to 3 days.

2. Roll the cheese mixture into 1-inch balls.

3. Roll the cheese balls in the pumpernickel crumbs and refrigerate until ready to serve, up to overnight.

Prizewinners

Gwendolyn Brooks won the Pulitzer Prize for her book of poems *Annie Allen* in 1950. She was the first African-American, male or female, to win a Pulitzer Prize.

Pearl Buck was awarded the Nobel Prize for Literature in 1938. She was the first American woman to win this honor and the only one until Toni Morrison in 1993.

Dorothy Parker's Cocktail Party

Dorothy Parker

The sharp-tongued Dorothy Parker was the only female founding member of the Algonquin Round Table, an intellectual literary circle formed by Robert Benchley, Robert Sherwood, James Thurber, and others at the Algonquin Hotel in New York City in June 1919. There was a lot of drinking at the Round Table, which did not slow down even when Prohibition tried to put a damper on social gatherings for over a decade in the 1920s and '30s. The Roaring Twenties roared loudest in New York with Dorothy's hedonistic circle of friends, who were movers and shakers of the stage and page. She partied in Bohemian Greenwich Village speakeasies and at Gatsby-esque house parties in Long Island mansions. Dorothy's high life was punctuated with lows that led her to several suicide attempts, which she eventually used as life-affirming subject material in her work, such as the poems "Re_sume_" and "The Flaw in Paganism."

Dorothy's illustrious literary career started with selling her poems to magazines. She also wrote captions for fashion photographs in *Vogue* and then became the drama critic for *Vanity Fair*. She began writing short stories and plays and then joined the staff of the newly formed *New Yorker* in 1925, contributing theater reviews and poetry. Her short stories and poems that were previously printed in magazines were collected and published in book form, starting with *Enough Rope*, in 1926. Her clever and cutting wit shines in these observations and social commentary on life and love. Later, she furnished book reviews for the *New Yorker* under the pseudonym "The Constant Reader" after she was no longer on the staff. Dorothy won the O. Henry Award for best short story of the year in 1929 for "The Big Blonde." That same year she went to Hollywood and worked as a screenwriter, eventually cowriting the screenplay of *A Star is Born* in 1937. Later in life, she worked as a book reviewer for *Esquire* magazine and was a visiting professor of English at California State College in LA before moving back to New York. Despite all the hard drinking, Dorothy lived into her mid seventies, unlike many of her Bohemian comrades. To buffer the alcohol, she must have eaten the bar snacks!

Round Table Bar Snacks

The following recipes are perfect snacks for the cocktail hour. Anything more elaborate would be dinner and not cocktail party fare. If your guests haven't had enough olives to eat in their martinis, the Olive Bites should satisfy them. When Dorothy Parker was a child, her favorite image of the city was when it was raining and the wet asphalt of the empty streets was "black and shining as ripe olives." (You can't have too many olive references for Dorothy Parker's Cocktail Party!) Cheese Straws are a portable hors d'oeuvre that are easy to nibble on while mingling, and Bar Nuts are a necessity to have stationed in strategic locations around the room in small bowls for guests to snack on during conversation. Pickled Dilly Green Beans may be used as a garnish for drinks such as

Bloody Marys and martinis, although some people enjoy them simply as crudités. The Volstead Act has long been repealed so there is no reason to serve your guests the sort of "bathtub gin" that Dorothy Parker and her friends had to endure. Pour triple-distilled vodka in your martinis and forego the cheap stuff. Your guests will thank you when they wake up with a less intense headache the next morning if they overindulge.

Olive Bites

SERVES 8

Note: this one requires a deep fat fryer or deep pot and cooking thermometer.

INGREDIENTS:

1 cup chopped black olives

½ cup chopped green olives

½ cup shredded cheddar cheese

¼ cup grated Asiago cheese

4 ounces softened cream cheese

¼ cup grated Parmesan cheese

½ cup flour, seasoned with salt, pepper, and cayenne pepper

2 eggs, beaten

1 cup Panko bread crumbs

4 cups peanut oil

METHOD:

1. Combine the olives with the cheddar, Asiago, and cream cheese and refrigerate for an hour.

2. Combine the bread crumbs with the Parmesan cheese.

3. Roll the olive mixture into 1-inch balls.

4. Roll the olive balls in the flour, then the eggs, and then the bread crumbs.

5. Refrigerate the coated olive balls for 30 minutes.

6. Heat the peanut oil to 365 degrees F in a deep fryer or deep pot on the stove.

7. Deep fry the olive balls for 3 minutes, until the coating is golden brown.

8. Drain the olive bites on paper towels and serve warm.

9. They may be reheated in a warm oven.

Cheese Straws

YEILDS 12

INGREDIENTS:

1 egg, beaten

2 sheets frozen puff pastry, thawed

½ cup shredded cheddar cheese

½ cup shredded Jarlsberg cheese

¼ cup grated Parmesan cheese

1 teaspoon celery seeds

1 tablespoon sesame seeds

1 teaspoon poppy seeds

½ teaspoon ground cayenne pepper

1 teaspoon paprika

METHOD:

1. Preheat the oven to 400 degrees F. Line 2 baking sheets with parchment paper.

2. Roll the puff pastry sheets out on a floured surface to make them a little larger and thinner. Set 1 sheet aside in the refrigerator.

3. Brush the sheet of pastry that is out with the beaten egg.

4. Sprinkle the cheeses, seeds, and seasonings evenly over the egg-washed pastry.

5. Get the other sheet of pastry out of the refrigerator and brush one side of it with the beaten egg.

6. Place the second piece of pastry, egg-wash side down, onto the cheese-covered pastry sheet. Press down gently on the top sheet of pastry to help the cheese adhere to the pastry inside.

7. With a pizza wheel or sharp knife, cut 1-inch wide strips lengthwise from the pastry.

8. Pick up each strip at the ends and twist several times and then set the straw on the prepared baking sheet and press down on the ends. Repeat with all of the strips, leaving a 1-inch space between them.

9. Refrigerate the straws for at least 15 minutes before baking. (They can also be frozen at this point and baked later.)

10. Bake the straws for 15 minutes. Remove them from the sheet pan when they have cooled.

Bar Nuts

Serves 8

Ingredients:

8 ounces whole almonds

8 ounces cashews

½ cup honey

2 teaspoons salt

2 teaspoons cumin

¼ teaspoon cayenne pepper

2 tablespoons vegetable oil

Method:

1. Preheat oven to 350 degrees F.

2. Toss the almonds and cashews in a bowl with the honey and oil.

3. Sprinkle the salt, cumin, and cayenne pepper over the nuts and toss to coat.

4. Bake 15 minutes, stir, and bake another 10 minutes until crisp and golden.

5. Cool and separate into individual nuts using oiled fingers.

6. Store in an airtight container.

Pickled Dilly Green Beans

YIELD 1 PINT

INGREDIENTS:

8 ounces fresh green beans

1 garlic clove

1 teaspoon dill seed

½ teaspoon cayenne pepper

1 tablespoon salt

½ cup cider vinegar

½ cup water

METHOD:

1. Wash the green beans and snap the stem ends off so the beans fit upright in a pint-size canning jar.

2. Put the garlic clove, dill seed, cayenne pepper, and salt in a pint-size canning jar.

3. Pack the beans upright in the canning jar.

4. Bring the water and vinegar to a boil and pour it into the jar over the beans leaving a ½-inch space at the top. (Add more vinegar and water if the beans are not covered completely.)

continued

5. Screw the lid on tightly and let the beans cool.

6. Let the beans pickle for one week (or up to one year). Refrigerate after opening.

7. Serve as a snack alone or on a relish tray, or use as a garnish for a Bloody Mary or martini.

"I like to have a martini
Two at the very most—
After three I'm under the table,
After four, I'm under my host."
— Dorothy Parker

Books by Dorothy Parker

Enough Rope (1926)
Sunset Gun (1927)
Laments for the Living (1930)
Death and Taxes (1931)
After Such Pleasures (1933)
Not So Deep as a Well (1936)
Here Lies (1939)

M.F.K. Fisher's Fireside Feast

Mary Frances Kennedy Fisher — 1908–1992

*"Sharing food with another human being is an intimate act
that should not be indulged in lightly."* — M.F.K. FISHER

Those words come from a prolific writer who shared her intimate food memories in a personal style that is inviting and irresistible. Mary Frances Kennedy Fisher's writings have influenced many chefs and food writers, elevating food writing to an art form praised beyond the realm of food professionals. She wrote passionately about subjects that were often simple things. Whether writing a sensual description of eating a juicy tangerine, describing the details in the preparation of a meal, or relating a divine restaurant experience, she recorded her discoveries in a style that allows us to experience life's simple pleasures through her eyes.

M.F.K. Fisher has been credited as the godmother of California Cuisine by Alice Waters, who was herself a pioneer in the movement with her Berkeley restaurant Chez Panisse. In a corporate chain-restaurant world where architectural presentations and a hodge-podge of sauces that fatigue the palate are the rule, Chez Panisse—the birthplace of California Cuisine—is a refreshing restaurant where simplicity is embraced. For example, strawberries and tomatoes are not a perpetual garnish, but they are featured prominently in the summer.

Produce is served only when it is in season at the peak of ripeness. The farm-to-restaurant connection that Alice and her colleagues have nurtured over the years enables the type of cooking where little embellishment is applied to the food so the virtue of the ingredients can shine through. I was working at Chez Panisse on the day that M.F.K. Fisher passed away, and with reverence we prepared selections from her works as part of the menu that evening. The printed menu of that June evening in 1992 hangs on the wall of my kitchen at home—a moment captured in time.

French Comfort Food

Consider a cozy three-course fireside feast with a few friends and a menu of simple French comfort foods satisfying to the body and soul, starting with French Onion Soup Gratinée. Continue the meal with a course of Escalloped Oysters, in honor of M.F.K. Fisher's book *Consider the Oyster*, and a green salad. For the dessert course, serve Individual Tarte Tatins drizzled with crème fraiche, a classic of French cuisine and in this case baked individually in muffin tins for an easy yet elegant presentation. Complete the meal with petits fours of Wolves Mouths, again in honor of one of Ms. Fisher's books *How to Cook a Wolf*, written in the midst of World War II when the wolf was truly at the door. Round out the evening with a nightcap of Cognac or dessert wine. M.F.K. Fisher liked to end her evenings watching the sunset from her porch, sipping her favorite mixture of white wine and Campari. I can't think of a more idyllic ending than that.

French Onion Soup Gratinée

SERVES 4

INGREDIENTS:

4 slices French bread

4 slices Provolone cheese

2 large onions

3 tablespoons unsalted butter

½ cup dry wine, white or red

32 ounces chicken broth (low salt)

2 sprigs fresh thyme

salt and pepper to taste

1 tablespoon Worcestershire sauce

2 tablespoons chopped fresh parsley

METHOD:

1. Preheat broiler.

2. Lay the French bread slices out on a baking pan. Top each slice of bread with a slice of Provolone cheese and place under the broiler until brown and bubbly. Set aside.

3. Slice the onions and caramelize them in the butter to a rich mahogany color.

continued

4. Add the wine to the onions, scraping up all the browned bits and cooking to make a reduction of caramelized onions.

5. Add the chicken broth and stir to combine with the onions. Add thyme, salt, and pepper and simmer for 45 minutes.

6. Remove the thyme sprigs, stir in the Worcestershire sauce, and ladle the soup into individual crocks.

7. Top each crock of soup with a cheesy bread slice.

8. Sprinkle with parsley.

Escalloped Oysters

SERVES 4

INGREDIENTS:

½ cup melted butter

1 cup soda cracker crumbs

½ cup bread crumbs

1 pint shucked oysters, drain and save the juice

¼ teaspoon salt

¼ teaspoon pepper

2 tablespoons cream

1 teaspoon lemon juice

1 teaspoon Worcestershire sauce

a few drops cayenne pepper sauce

METHOD:

1. Preheat oven to 425 degrees F. Butter a baking dish.

2. In a bowl, toss together the melted butter, cracker crumbs, and bread crumbs. Spread half of this mixture on the bottom of the prepared baking dish.

3. Arrange the oysters on top of the crumb mixture and sprinkle them with salt and pepper.

4. Mix the cream, lemon juice, Worcestershire sauce, cayenne pepper sauce, and 3 tablespoons oyster juice together and pour this mixture over the oysters.

5. Sprinkle the remaining crumb mixture over the oysters and bake for 25 minutes.

Individual Tarte Tatins

SERVES 4

INGREDIENTS:

1 apple, peeled, cored, and quartered

1 sheet frozen puff pastry, thawed

8 teaspoons butter

16 teaspoons brown sugar

crème fraiche

METHOD:

1. Preheat oven to 375 degrees F.

2. Put 1 teaspoon butter and 2 teaspoons brown sugar in the bottom of 8 muffin-tin cups.

3. Cut each apple quarter in half crosswise and place each apple chunk on top of the brown sugar and butter in the muffin-tin cups.

4. Bake the apples for 12 minutes.

5. While the apples are baking, cut eight 3-inch rounds out of the puff pastry. Poke holes in each circle with a fork.

6. After the apples have baked for 12 minutes, remove them from the oven, place the pastry rounds on top of the apples, and return them to the oven to bake for 15 minutes more.

7. Remove the pan from the oven, invert it onto a baking pan, and let it rest for 5 minutes to allow the fruit and caramel to glaze the top of the tarts.

8. Remove the muffin-tin pan and serve the tarts warm, with a dollop of crème fraiche, two per person.

Wolves Mouths

SERVES 4

INGREDIENTS:

½ cup dried cherries

¼ cup apple juice

¼ cup Amaretto

8 ounces almond paste

1 egg white

METHOD:

1. Preheat oven to 325 degrees F.

2. Soak the dried cherries in the apple juice and Amaretto while preparing the dough.

3. Combine the almond paste and egg white in a food processor until smooth. Add more egg white if necessary to make a smooth, stiff paste.

4. Put the mixture in a pastry bag with a large star tip.

5. Pipe little star kisses onto a parchment paper-lined cookie sheet in rows.

6. Drain the cherries and place one on top of the middle of each cookie to resemble a howling wolf's mouth.

7. Bake for 12 minutes. Peel off the paper and cool.

"Gastronomical perfection can be reached in these combinations: one person dining alone, usually upon a couch or a hillside; two persons, of no matter what sex or age, dining in a good restaurant; six people, of no matter what sex or age, dining in a good home." — M.F.K. Fisher

Some of M.F.K. Fisher's Books

Serve It Forth (1937)

Consider the Oyster (1941)

How to Cook a Wolf (1942)

The Gastronomical Me (1943)

An Alphabet for Gourmets (1949)

The Art of Eating (1954)

The Story of Wine in California (1962)

Map of Another Town: A Memoir of Provence (1964)

The Cooking of Provincial France (1968)

With Bold Knife and Fork (1969)

Among Friends (1970)

Two Towns in Provence (1983)

Long Ago in France: The Years in Dijon (1991)

To Begin Again: Stories and Memoirs 1908–1929 (1992)

Stay Me, Oh Comfort Me: Journals and Stories 1933–1941 (1993)

Last House: Reflections, Dreams and Observations 1943–1991 (1995)

The Dark Side of Wild Women

The Bacchae

The Bacchae is an ancient Greek tragedy by the playwright Euripides where the short version of the lesson learned too late is this: Don't mess with the women on the hill when they are partying! Euripides chose women as his subjects more often than the other Greek playwrights and taunted the traditional hero glorification. He was a realist who liked to show people as they really were—tragic flaws and all. He wrote shockers, choosing to enact the moments of the hero/heroine's decay and disintegration. (*Medea* is a perfect example of this, where Medea kills her own children to get back at Jason, her cheating husband of Golden Fleece fame.) In *The Bacchae*, the women of the town are temporarily Bacchantes, followers of Bacchus (or Dionysus) the god of wine, and they are engaged in an orgiastic ritual dedicated to him. The Bacchantes' ritual involves working themselves into a frenzy by drinking wine and dancing to drumbeats, rocking their heads back and forth to induce a euphoric state of mind. Think of it as the original version of a rave.

The revelers become enthusiastic, which means in Greek that the god is within them. In this case, the god influencing them is tricky and formidable, with vengeance on his agenda. In this tragedy, things go wrong for everyone when the son of one of the Bacchantes tries to spy on the raving women by disguising himself as one of them and infiltrating the "festival." The enthusiastic state of the women drives them to tear apart the interloper and feast on his raw flesh, and then his own mother parades his head back into town on an ivy-twined stick. The ivy-twined stick is known as a thyrsus, which is normally topped with a pinecone, not a human head. It is supposed to be used as an instrument of celebration, not horror. When the women come back to their senses and realize what they have done, it is a tragic realization for the whole town that one does not taunt the gods, especially Bacchus, who has had the last word.

Halloween Party

Your Halloween party doesn't have to be as sinister as *The Bacchae*, but the horror story is perfect for a play reading if you're feeling thespian. The following recipes will set the right mood. For your flesh-eating friends, there is a recipe for Meat-Basting Sauce. If you prefer authenticity and would like to indulge in omophagia (eating raw flesh), may I suggest sushi, steak tartar, or carpaccio? Stuffed Artichokes are meant to symbolize the thyrsus in the play as artichokes resemble the pinecone on top of the ceremonial staff. There are Potato Ghosts because every Halloween party needs ghosts, and there are Bones of the Dead, which are actually delicious almond cookies that resemble bleached bones—you can stack them up into a bone pile. Offer wine to your guests to appease Bacchus, or you don't know what might happen!

Meat-Basting Sauce

YIELD 2 CUPS

INGREDIENTS:

2 ounces butter

1 tablespoon olive oil

2 minced garlic cloves

1 cup Worcestershire sauce

¼ cup sherry

1 tablespoon honey

½ cup water

1 teaspoon celery salt

1 teaspoon onion powder

METHOD:

1. Sauté garlic in butter and olive oil for 2 minutes.

2. Add the remaining ingredients and simmer for 15 minutes.

3. Use for basting grilled steak, ribs, or chicken.

Stuffed Artichokes

SERVES 8

INGREDIENTS:

1 lemon

2 cups dry bread crumbs

½ cup grated Parmesan cheese

2 cloves garlic, minced

¼ cup chopped parsley

¼ cup chopped, cooked bacon

¼ cup olive oil

1 teaspoon salt

¼ teaspoon pepper

4 whole artichokes

½ cup white wine

1½ cups water

METHOD:

1. Grate the zest of the lemon and cut the lemon in half and set aside.

2. Mix the lemon zest with the bread crumbs, Parmesan cheese, garlic, parsley, bacon, olive oil, salt, and pepper. Set aside.

3.   Prepare the artichokes for stuffing by cutting the stems off the bottoms first. As you cut the artichokes, rub the lemon on all of the cut places to prevent browning.

4.   Cut the top inch off of each artichoke with a serrated knife and rub the lemon on the cut. Discard the cut off part.

5.   Snip the thorny tips off the remaining leaves and rub with the lemon.

6.   Pull out the center leaves to expose the fuzzy choke in the center, and then scoop out the choke with a melon baller. Squeeze lemon juice into the center of each artichoke.

7.   Spoon some of the bread crumb stuffing into the center of each artichoke and then pack the rest of the stuffing down in between each leaf.

8.   Pour the water and white wine into the bottom of a large pot.

9.   Place a steamer rack in the bottom of the pot and put the artichokes on the rack.

10. Cover the pot with a tight-fitting lid and simmer for 50 minutes until a leaf can be pulled easily from an artichoke.

11. Remove artichokes from steamer, cut in half, and arrange on a platter.

Potato Ghosts

SERVES 8

INGREDIENTS:

2 pounds potatoes, peeled and cut into chunks

2 ounces butter

salt and white pepper to taste

pinch nutmeg

1 egg yolk

1 egg

1 tablespoon black sesame seeds

METHOD:

1. Preheat oven to 425 degrees F.

2. Put potatoes in cold, salted water and bring to a boil. Simmer until tender, about 15 minutes. Drain and let the steam escape.

3. Mash the potatoes and mix in the butter. Season to taste with salt, white pepper, and nutmeg.

4. Beat in the egg yolk and egg.

5. Put the potato mixture in a pastry bag with no tip.

6. Pipe the potato mixture onto a parchment paper-lined baking sheet in a straight upward motion and release straight up to make 3-inch-high ghosts. Place 2 sesame seeds near the top for "eyes."

7. Brown the potatoes in the oven for 5 minutes.

8. Cool enough to handle and lift the ghosts off the paper and place them on a warm platter.

Bones of the Dead

SERVES 8

INGREDIENTS:

1 cup sugar

¾ teaspoon lemon juice

½ teaspoon baking powder

   pinch of salt

1 egg

⅔ cup flour

⅔ cup almonds, finely chopped

METHOD:

1. Preheat oven to 350 degrees F.

2. Combine the sugar, lemon juice, baking powder, and salt with an electric mixer.

3. Add the egg and mix until spongy.

4. Add the flour and almonds and mix briefly, just enough for the dough to come together.

5. On a floured surface, roll the dough into ropes the thickness of a pencil with your hands.

6. Cut the ropes into 3-inch lengths and put them on a parchment paper-lined baking sheet, leaving an inch between them to expand.

7. Bake for 12–15 minutes.

8. Cool before removing from the paper.

Nellie Melba's Hand

Peach Melba is a classic dessert made of peaches and raspberries and named in honor of a famous opera star. For Halloween, create a gory interpretation of the classic by making a peach gelatin that is garnished with raspberries. First, fold 1 cup sweetened whipped cream into a 3-ounce box of peach gelatin mixed with 1/2 cup boiling water and 5 ice cubes. Next, pour the mixture into a washed and oiled latex glove, tie a knot in the glove, and refrigerate it flat. When set, cut and peel off the glove and set the hand on a platter lined with lettuce leaves. Put sliced almonds on the fingertips for fingernails and pour sweetened frozen raspberries around the wrist. The raspberries will thaw into a pool of clotted "blood." Makes a hand-y centerpiece!

Bridget's Jonesing for Chocolate Soiree

Driven to the Edge of Reason for Chocolate

In the novel *Bridget Jones's Diary* by Helen Fielding, a British woman is determined to improve herself while she looks for love during a year in which she keeps a personal diary and records such details as how many cigarettes she smoked and when she smoked them. (The sequel, *Bridget Jones: The Edge of Reason*, continues the saga.) Bridget tries to modify her behavior through self-improvement rituals such as dieting, but all she really needs to do is indulge in a bite of chocolate now and then for that sense of well-being she is seeking. Chocolate releases endorphins in the brain, bathing neurons in the chemical and inducing in the consumer of the cocoa bean the same state of euphoria as the feeling of falling in love. That is why some say chocolate is better than sex! Experts say that eating chocolate is healthy for you because it contains antioxidants (especially dark chocolate), which can help reduce the presence of free-radicals that damage cells and DNA. Moderation is important though because chocolate is high in saturated fat and calories, so it is better for you (and more satisfying) to eat a few bites of good quality chocolate than it is to eat a whole pound of the cheap stuff. Cocoa powder has no fat or sugar in it so it can be enjoyed with more abandon as an ingredient in beverages and foods. Sometimes moderation has no place, such as holiday time, so indulge and diet later. Quality of life is a balancing act.

The cocoa tree is named *theobroma cacao*, theobroma being Greek for "food of the gods." (Angel food cake has its virtues, but evidently chocolate is what they preferred on Mount Olympus!) *Theobroma cacao* is an evergreen that thrives up to twenty degrees north and south of the equator, grows approximately twenty feet tall, and produces pods from six to ten inches long containing twenty to forty beans, each about an inch long. The cocoa pods are harvested year-round, though mostly from May to December. The first step to making chocolate is the fermentation of the beans and pulp which are removed from the pod and left in the sun for a few days. The beans are later cleaned, dried, and shipped to other countries. Once there, the beans are roasted at 250 degrees Fahrenheit for about an hour and cracked open, and the kernels (called "nibs") are separated from the shell. The nibs are ground to form liquid called chocolate liquor which is largely made up of protein and carbohydrates suspended in oil. A second grinding between sets of rollers reduces the nibs to a more desirable size from which chocolate can be made by adding sugar, more cocoa butter, and milk solids for milk chocolate and mixed in a process called conching. White chocolate is simply a cocoa butter and sugar mixture that lacks the dark cocoa component.

A Chocolate Soiree

If you are "Jonesing" for a chocolate fix, use the following recipes to host a party where the cocoa bean is the star. Start your soiree with a cup of Hot Malted White Chocolate for everyone, entertain your guests with a chocolate-based movie, and feed them chicken covered in mole sauce, a savory Mexican sauce made with chocolate. Follow the meal with a dessert buffet tantalizing enough to tempt the gods down from Mount Olympus, featuring Chocolate Turtle Brownie Cups, Chocolate Mousse Cheesecake, Chocolate Mousse, Chocolate Crème Brulee, and a chocolate fountain. Add sweetened cocoa powder to your whipped cream for extra points!

Hot Malted White Chocolate

Ingredients:

10 cups milk

6 ounces white chocolate, chopped or chips

1½ cups malted milk powder

⅔ cup brown sugar

1 tablespoon vanilla

freshly grated nutmeg

Method:

1. Heat the milk to a simmer in a saucepan and remove from heat. Put 2 cups of milk in a blender.

2. Add the white chocolate to the milk in the saucepan and whisk to melt and combine.

3. Add the brown sugar, malted milk powder, and vanilla to the pan and whisk to combine.

4. Divide the hot white chocolate milk mixture among 12 mugs.

5. Blend the milk in the blender to make it froth and divide the frothy milk among the mugs.

6. Garnish each mug with freshly grated nutmeg.

Chocolate Turtle Brownie Cups

SERVES 12

INGREDIENTS:

1 cup caramels, unwrapped

¼ cup cream

1 package brownie mix
   brownie mix requirements (egg,
   oil, water)

1 cup chopped pecans

½ cup chocolate chips

METHOD:

1. Preheat oven to 350 degrees F and oil a muffin tin.

2. Melt caramels and cream together in a saucepan over low heat. Stir to combine and set aside.

continued

3. Prepare the brownie mix as directed and divide it evenly in the muffin tin.

4. Sprinkle half of the pecans and all of the chocolate chips on top of the brownie mix in the cups and bake as directed, about 15 minutes.

5. Remove from the oven and spoon a teaspoon of melted caramel in the middle of each brownie cup.

6. Sprinkle the remaining pecans on the caramel and let the brownie cups cool. Remove from the muffin tin and serve.

Chocolate Mousse Cheesecake

SERVES 12

INGREDIENTS:

2 cups chocolate cookie crumbs

2 cups sugar

¼ cup melted butter

24 ounces cream cheese, softened

2 tablespoons cornstarch

3 eggs

8 ounces dark chocolate, melted

1½ cups sour cream

1 teaspoon vanilla

chocolate mousse (recipe follows)

2 cups sweetened whipped cream

grated chocolate bar

METHOD:

1. Preheat oven to 350 degrees F.

2. In a bowl combine cookie crumbs, ½ cup sugar, and the melted butter with a rubber spatula. Press the mixture into the bottom of a springform pan that has been sprayed with oil and bake for 12 minutes. Remove from oven and set aside.

3. With an electric mixer, beat the cream cheese until fluffy. Add 1½ cups sugar and, cornstarch and cream together. Beat in eggs one at a time, scraping down the bowl after each one.

4. Mix in the melted chocolate until smooth. Stir in the sour cream and vanilla.

5. Pour this batter into the springform pan and bake for 1 hour. Remove from the oven and cool at room temperature and then chill completely.

6. Top the chilled cheesecake with the chocolate mousse and smooth it out.

7. Top the chocolate mousse with whipped cream and garnish with grated chocolate.

Chocolate Mousse

SERVES 12

INGREDIENTS:

12 ounces semisweet chocolate chips

4 egg whites

2 whole eggs

4 egg yolks

¾ cup heavy cream

METHOD:

1. Melt the chocolate in a metal or glass bowl set over hot but not boiling water. When melted, remove the bowl from heat and set aside.

2. Whip the egg whites to stiff peaks with a wire whisk or electric mixer; set aside.

3. Crack the whole eggs into the egg yolks and beat well to combine. Stir the yolk mixture into the melted chocolate.

4. Fold the whipped egg whites into the chocolate/yolk mixture with a rubber spatula.

5. Whip the heavy cream to soft peaks and whisk half of it into the chocolate/egg mixture to lighten it. Then, gently fold the remaining whipped cream in, just to incorporate. Chill to set at least 2 hours before serving.

Note: Use pasteurized eggs if you are concerned about salmonella in raw eggs.

Chocolate Crème Brulée

SERVES 12

INGREDIENTS:

2 cups half-and-half

4 cups cream

1 cup sugar

2 tablespoons cocoa powder

12 ounces semisweet chocolate, melted

12 egg yolks

1 teaspoon vanilla

1 tablespoon coffee liqueur (optional)

   granulated sugar for caramelizing

METHOD:

1. Preheat oven to 325 degrees F. Put twelve 4-ounce ramekins in a large 2-inch deep baking dish and set aside. (Use 2 baking pans, if necessary.)

2. In a saucepan, heat the half-and-half, cream, and sugar to melt the sugar. Stir in the cocoa powder and melted chocolate and remove from heat.

3. Mix the egg yolks, vanilla, and coffee liqueur in a bowl. Whisk the hot cream mixture into the egg yolks and then strain the resulting custard into a pitcher.

4. Pour the hot custard into the ramekins, dividing it evenly. Pour hot water in the baking dish around the ramekins to come halfway up the ramekins. Cover the baking dish tightly with foil.

5. Bake for 30 minutes and check to see if the custard is set. Carefully jiggle the pan and if the custard is not set, cover and bake for 10 minutes more. Remove from oven and then remove the ramekins from the water bath to cool. Refrigerate until completely chilled, about 2 hours.

6. To caramelize, sprinkle the top of the custard with sugar and use a propane torch to caramelize the sugar. If you don't have a torch to caramelize the sugar, serve with whipped cream on top instead.

Movies to Eat Chocolate By

These choco-centric movies were all books first:

Like Water for Chocolate (1992) by Laura Esquivel

Chocolat (2000) by Joanne Harris

Charlie and the Chocolate Factory (2005) by Roald Dahl

Willie Wonka and the Chocolate Factory (1971) by Roald Dahl

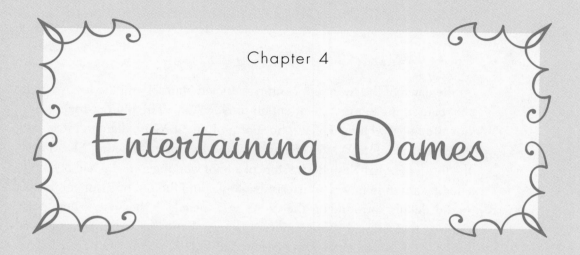

Chapter 4

Entertaining Dames

A Florodora Girl's After-Hours Dinner Party

Evelyn Nesbit

At the dawn of the twentieth century, a society murder and the love triangle that caused it captured the attention of New York. The murder trial of millionaire outcast Harry Thaw, who shot prominent Manhattan architect and party gent Stanford White, centered on the testimony of young Mrs. Thaw, the former Evelyn Nesbit. The story of a poor working girl who had been rescued by a rich man was an irresistible topic, and the public's hunger for the sordid details surrounding the crime was fueled by the new yellow press tabloids that printed sensationalized stories about this soap opera of love, money, and social class. Long before the O.J. Simpson trial, even before Clarence Darrow's infamous Leopold and Loeb case, twentieth-century America obsessed over the beautiful showgirl in the middle of the Stanford White murder in 1906.

Evelyn Nesbit spent her childhood in poverty in Pittsburgh, Pennsylvania, after her father died when she was eight years old. In 1899, the Nesbit family moved to Philadelphia, where Evelyn and her mother both worked at Wanamaker's Department Store. Barely able to make ends meet, Evelyn accepted an offer to pose as a model for a portrait, thus changing the course of her life in a trajectory toward fame, fortune, and tragedy. Evelyn's virtuous image appeared in books and magazines, and after she modeled for a year for commercial illustrators in Philadelphia, the Nesbits moved to New York City to seek their fortune. In New York, Evelyn posed for photographers as well as artists. Newspapers had just begun printing photographs and Evelyn's made her an overnight sensation. Her fame helped land her a part in the hit Broadway musical *Florodora*, in which she played a small but prominent role as a Spanish dancer.

Now a showgirl, sixteen-year-old Evelyn attracted the attention of Stanford White, a wealthy architect who had redesigned the interior of Teddy Roosevelt's White House and designed New York landmarks such as Madison Square Garden and the Washington Square Arch, as well as luxurious mansions for the nouveau riche. Forty-seven years old and married, Stanford started an affair with Evelyn that would ultimately cost him his life. The affair began in his apartment in the tower above Madison Square Garden where he often hosted intimate dinner parties and entertained young showgirls on a red velvet swing. According to Evelyn, he perched her, stark naked, on the swing and pushed her until she was swinging high enough to kick her foot through a paper parasol mounted on the ceiling. Stanford spent most nights out on the town, starting with drinks at a private club. The Players, a club for theater people was his favorite. Later, he would typically have dinner with friends at Delmonico's, followed by a visit to a show, music hall, boxing match, or the opera.

The decadent lifestyle that Stanford White led was typical of the turn-of-the-century wealthy elite New York male, and Evelyn was not the only showgirl on his plate. Evelyn decided to make Stanford jealous and started seeing other men, eventually marrying Harry Thaw, the heir to a Pittsburgh railroad fortune.

Thaw was shunned from New York parties because of his antisocial, bizarre behavior and mood swings. He had no real friends so he had to buy them. He was extremely jealous that his wife and Stanford White had been lovers and he beat a confession out of her about the details of her lost virginity. Thaw despised White's popularity and his decadent ways, and his jealousy over his wife's former affair with the architect boiled over into murder in 1906. White was shot and killed by Thaw in the rooftop cabaret at Madison Square Garden, ironically an entertainment complex of White's own creation. Evelyn testified in court that she had once been given drugged Champagne by Stanford White in his apartment and that she later woke up naked in bed. Thaw's defense said that this information had driven him crazy and led to his shooting of White. Propaganda on sheet music and postcards in Harry Thaw's defense saying "For the sake of wife and home" was circulated and it was rumored that Evelyn had been paid off by the Thaw family for her testimony. Thaw was found not guilty by reason of insanity and sent to a prison for the criminally insane. Moral reformists called Thaw a hero in the struggle over vice. Evelyn Nesbit, the center of the storm, was divorced by Thaw after his release and her star fell to the level of being a dancer on the vaudeville circuit. But her role in the Thaw-White murder lives on, documented in the tabloid press that exposed the conflicts over morality between the rich and the middle class at the beginning of the twentieth century.

After-Theatre Dinner Party

The following recipes for Lobster Newburg, Delmonico Steak, and Delmonico Potatoes were inventions and menu standards of New York City's first luxury restaurant. Delmonico's set the standard for gourmet food in the late 1800s. You can create a fin de siècle dinner party with this rich surf and turf menu to be enjoyed after an opulent night out at the theatre. Serve Champagne with the dessert of Red Velvet Swing Cake in honor of Evelyn Nesbit, the *Florodora* girl who brought down the house at Madison Square Garden in 1906.

Lobster Newburg

SERVES 4

INGREDIENTS:

4 cooked lobster tails

1 minced shallot

3 ounces unsalted butter

1 cup cream

1 ounce Madeira wine

1 egg yolk

salt and pepper to taste

dash cayenne pepper sauce

METHOD:

1. Remove the lobster tails from their shells and cut the meat into slices.

2. Sauté the shallots and lobster slices in 2 ounces of butter.

continued

3. Add ½ cup cream and reduce by half.

4. Add the Madeira wine and cook a minute to burn off the alcohol. It may ignite and produce a flame that will die down and extinguish itself.

5. Whisk the remaining cream and egg yolk together and add it to the pan. Swirl over low heat for a few minutes to thicken.

6. Add the remaining butter, salt, pepper, and cayenne pepper sauce, stir and then remove from heat.

7. Serve immediately.

Delmonico Steak

SERVES 4

INGREDIENTS:

4 New York strip steaks, boneless

   salt and pepper

METHOD:

1. Preheat broiler.

2. Sprinkle salt and pepper on the steaks.

3. Broil 5 minutes on each side for medium.

Delmonico Potatoes

SERVES 4

INGREDIENTS:

2 pounds potatoes, peeled and cubed

2 ounces melted butter

2 ounces lemon juice

2 tablespoons chopped parsley

salt and pepper to taste

METHOD:

1. Put the potatoes in cold salted water to cover.

2. Bring to a boil and simmer until tender, about 15 minutes.

3. Drain the potatoes.

continued

4.   Toss the warm potatoes with melted butter, lemon juice, and parsley.

5.   Season to taste with salt and pepper.

Red Velvet Swing Cake

SERVES 8

INGREDIENTS:

Cake:

2 tablespoons unsweetened cocoa powder

2 ounces red food coloring

1 cup buttermilk

1 teaspoon salt

1 teaspoon vanilla extract

4 ounces soft unsalted butter

1½ cups sugar

2 eggs

2½ cups flour

1½ teaspoons baking soda

1 teaspoon white vinegar

Frosting:

2 cans of cream cheese frosting

Garnish:

  fresh strawberries

METHOD:

1. Preheat oven to 350 degrees F and grease two 9-inch round cake pans.

2. Make a paste of cocoa and food coloring. Set aside.

3. Combine the buttermilk, salt, and 1 teaspoon vanilla. Set aside.

4. In a large bowl, cream together the butter and sugar until light and fluffy. Beat in the eggs one at a time and then stir in the cocoa mixture.

5. Beat in the buttermilk mixture alternately with the flour, mixing just until incorporated. Stir together baking soda and vinegar and then gently fold it into the cake batter.

6. Pour the batter into the prepared pans and bake for 30 minutes, or until a toothpick inserted into the center of the cake comes out clean. Cool completely before frosting.

7. Frost and stack the layers of cake and then frost the entire outside of the cake with the cream cheese frosting.

8. Decorate the frosted cake with sliced strawberries.

Sister Evelyn

Theodore Dreiser's novel *Sister Carrie*, published in 1900, tells the story of a Chicago shopgirl's rise to fame and fortune from New York showgirl to Broadway star, and simultaneously recounts the tale of her wealthy lover's demise. Interestingly, the real-life Evelyn Nesbit's rise and Stanford White's ultimate demise mirror the novel in theme and setting, proving that life indeed imitates art sometimes!

Gibson Girl

Evelyn Nesbit was one of the models who posed for illustrator Charles Dana Gibson, who created the image of the virtuous independent American woman, known as the "Gibson Girl," for magazines. Gibson's drawing of Evelyn, titled "Women: the Eternal Question," was published in 1905 and shows her profile with long hair streaming down to form a question mark.

A Rodeo Queen's Wild West Barbecue

Annie Oakley

Annie Oakley was born Phoebe Moses, in a log cabin on the Ohio frontier in 1860. At age sixteen, she entered a shooting contest in Cincinnati against accomplished marksman and vaudevillian Frank E. Butler and won the match. She later married Frank and together they joined Buffalo Bill Cody's traveling Wild West Show in 1885. For seventeen years Annie was the star attraction, winning awards and captivating audiences around the world with her sharp-shooting skills. Marvelous feats with pistols, rifles, and shotguns made Annie a legend in her own time. At a distance of ninety feet, Annie could shoot a play-ing card with its thin side facing her and then puncture holes in it five or six times as it fell to the ground.

In her act she shot the ashes off a cigarette held in her husband's mouth, which prompted the crowned head of Germany to request that she do the same with him when the show traveled to Europe. Queen Victoria was also impressed with Annie's skills when the Wild West Show was entertaining in England as part of the Queen's Golden Jubilee. The five-foot-tall markswoman was called "Little Sure Shot" by Sitting Bull, who was also part of Buffalo Bill's Wild West Show. Thomas Edison captured Annie's shooting skills on film and turned them into nickelodeon pieces. With her talent and determination,

Buckeye native Annie Oakley broke barriers for women, showing that a woman could compete and succeed in a man's world.

Western Barbecue

A western barbecue is all about meat: beef brisket, pork ribs, and smoked sausage being the holy trinity of BBQ in Texas, for instance. Follow the recipe for Cowgirl Brisket Rub and you will have a taste of what Annie Oakley's cowboy and Indian Wild West Show colleagues may have eaten on the frontier before their show business days. Chuck Wagon Beans and Potato Salad are the humble accompaniments to be served with barbecued brisket, and a sweet ending of buckeyes, the unofficial state candy of Ohio, pays tribute to Annie Oakley's buckeye roots.

Cowgirl Brisket Rub

YIELD 1/2 CUP

INGREDIENTS:

1 tablespoon onion powder

1 tablespoon garlic powder

1 tablespoon paprika

1 teaspoon celery salt

3 teaspoons salt

2 teaspoons sugar

2 teaspoons pepper

2 teaspoons dried oregano

1 teaspoon liquid smoke

prepared barbecue sauce

METHOD:

1. Mix all ingredients together.

2. Use to rub on whole beef brisket, let sit in refrigerator overnight.

3. Oven roast or grill the brisket at 275 degrees F 30 minutes per pound.

4. Let brisket sit for 15 minutes, then slice across the grain.

   Serve with barbecue sauce.

Chuck Wagon Beans

SERVES 6

INGREDIENTS:

1 slice bacon, chopped

½ cup diced onion

1 minced garlic clove

1 cup tomato sauce

1 cup water

¼ cup brown sugar

1 teaspoon Dijon mustard

2 tablespoons molasses

1 tablespoon honey

2 tablespoons cider vinegar

2 cups cooked pinto beans (canned is okay)

1 cup cooked kidney beans (canned is okay)

1 cup cooked cannellini beans (canned is okay)

½ teaspoon cayenne pepper sauce

salt and pepper to taste

METHOD:

1. Cook bacon, onion, and garlic together in a pot for 5 minutes.

2. Add the tomato sauce, water, brown sugar, Dijon mustard, molasses, honey, and vinegar and bring to a boil. Simmer 5 minutes.

3. Stir in the beans and simmer until the liquid thickens, about **20** minutes.

4. Season with salt, pepper, and cayenne pepper sauce.

Potato Salad

SERVES 6

INGREDIENTS:

3 pounds potatoes, scrubbed

1 cup mayonnaise

½ cup sour cream

1 cup mayonnaise-style salad dressing

¾ cup minced white onion

¼ cup chopped pimentos

¼ cup pickle relish

salt and pepper to taste

METHOD:

1. Boil the potatoes with their skins on until cooked.

2. Drain potatoes and in a big bowl mash them slightly into chunks.

3. Add the rest of the ingredients and toss to combine.

4. Chill until ready to serve.

Buckeyes

Yield 2 dozen

Ingredients:

8 ounces powdered sugar

5 ounces creamy peanut butter

4 ounces soft butter

8 ounces semisweet chocolate chips

1½ teaspoons vegetable shortening (without trans fats, please)

1 bamboo skewer

Method:

1. Mix the powdered sugar, peanut butter, and butter together.

2. Roll the mixture into 1-inch balls and place on a cookie sheet. Put in freezer while melting the chocolate.

3. Melt the chocolate and shortening together in a double boiler.

4. Remove the peanut butter balls from the freezer and dip them one by one into the melted chocolate with the bamboo skewer. Dip only ¾ in, leaving a circle of exposed peanut butter on the top to resemble a buckeye.

5. Place the dipped candies on wax paper and smooth out the holes left from the bamboo skewer.

6. Place the buckeye candies in the refrigerator to harden the chocolate.

Women of the American West

Lotta Crabtree performed at eight years old in the mining camps of the California Gold Rush in the Sierra Mountains. Her mother collected the gold nuggets that were thrown on the stage at the little dancer. She became a famous San Francisco stage actress as an adult and moved to New York to perform on Broadway.

. . .

Calamity Jane was a rowdy Indian scout with General Custer who drank, dressed, and shot like a man. She performed in Buffalo Bill Cody's Wild West Show for a short time. She is buried in Deadwood, South Dakota, next to the love of her life, Wild Bill Hickok.

It's Relative

My grandmother, Florence Sager, is a descendant of Catherine Sager's family, who emigrated West on the Oregon Trail with her family in the early 1800s. Along the way, both of Catherine's parents died, orphaning the seven Sager children, including a baby born on the Trail. The children made it to Oregon only to be attacked by Indians when they were staying with missionary Narcissa Whitman. The Whitman massacre claimed the lives of some of Catherine's siblings, but she survived to tell of the tragedy.

Check This Out:

National Cowgirl Museum and Hall of Fame
1720 Gendy Street
Fort Worth, Texas 76107
www.cowgirl.net

French Quarter Fat Tuesday

Ellen DeGeneres

A native daughter of New Orleans, Louisiana, Ellen DeGeneres is a queen of several things: comedy, "coming out," and dancing. She currently hosts *The Ellen DeGeneres Show*, a talk show complete with an in-house DJ for her dancing whims. Her "coming out" as a lesbian on her television show *Ellen* in 1997 created a national frenzy, getting her on the cover of *Time* magazine and thrusting her into the harsh spotlight of critics, including some of her show's advertisers who pulled their support.

All of this drama was preceded by the average life of a girl from New Orleans who once painted houses and shucked oysters for a living. Stand-up comedy was her passion and in 1985 she entered the San Francisco Stand-Up Comedy Competition, taking second prize. (Sinbad took first.) From there she appeared on the *Tonight Show* with Johnny Carson, and in 1994 she played the role of a bookstore employee on an ABC sitcom. The next year the show was renamed *Ellen* and she became a household name with the show's popularity and subsequent controversy. Ellen hosted the 2001 Emmys, and played the voice of Dory in the 2003 animated film *Finding Nemo*.

Mardi Gras Dessert Party

In New Orleans, Mardi Gras is a tradition featuring spectacular balls, parades, and revelry. The oft-repeated tagline heard during the festivities,

"laissez les bons temps rouler," means "let the good times roll" in French. Mardi Gras, French for "Fat Tuesday," is a celebration of indulging the flesh, with the apex being the day before Ash Wednesday when the fun must come to a screeching halt for the Catholic season of Lent. Rio de Janeiro's Carnaval and Venice's Carnevale are both pre-Lenten festivals also dedicated to the same purpose. The word carnival has the Latin root "carne" which means flesh, and "vale" added means a "farewell to the flesh." Different types of indulging (and overindulging!) of the flesh take place during Mardi Gras: drinking alcohol, feasting, dancing, and exposing body parts for beads.

The following recipes are no less indulgent in the flesh for a Mardi Gras Dessert Party. A tribute to Ole Man River, whose mouth dumps the silt from the entire Midwest into the Gulf of Mexico at the city of New Orleans, Mississippi Mud Marshmallow Brownies mimic the Mississippi delta and the surrounding bayous in texture and color only! A gooey marshmallow layer is situated on top of a rich chocolate brownie base with a fudgy glaze on top. This is the sweetest marsh you'll ever sink your teeth into. Pecan Pralines in the French Quarter are equivalent to fudge on Mackinac Island or salt water taffy at the boardwalk in Ocean City. Make a batch of the sugary morsels along with Bananas Foster, a flambé dessert invented in New Orleans. No Mardi Gras celebration is complete without a King Cake decorated in gold, purple, and green. King Cake Trifle is a twist on the classic, complete with the plastic baby doll inside.

Mississippi Mud Marshmallow Brownies

SERVES 6

INGREDIENTS:

1 package brownie mix
   brownie mix requirements (egg,
   oil, water)

12 ounces marshmallow cream

1 cup cream

1 cup chocolate chips

METHOD:

1. Preheat oven to 350 degrees F.

2. Prepare the brownie mix as directed and pour it into a greased
    8 x 11-inch pan.

3. Bake according to the directions on the package.

4. Remove from the oven and spread the marshmallow cream over the
    brownies. Let cool.

5. Melt the chocolate chips in the cream over low heat and stir to combine.
    Pour the melted chocolate mixture over the cooled marshmallow cream
    and let cool completely before cutting into squares.

Pecan Pralines

YIELD 2 DOZEN

INGREDIENTS:

1 cup brown sugar

2 cups sugar

4 ounces butter

2 tablespoons corn syrup

1 cup milk

4 cups pecans

METHOD:

1. Mix the brown sugar, sugar, butter, corn syrup, and milk together in a 3-quart saucepan and bring to a boil.

2. Simmer for 20 minutes, stirring occasionally.

3. Add pecans and continue cooking until a candy thermometer reads 234 degrees F.

4. Stir the mixture and then drop by tablespoons onto waxed paper and let pralines harden.

5. When cool, store in an airtight container, or wrap individually in plastic.

Bananas Foster

SERVES 6

INGREDIENTS:

5 firm ripe bananas

2 ounces unsalted butter

½ cup brown sugar

¼ cup orange juice

1 ounce Myers's dark rum

6 scoops vanilla ice cream

METHOD:

1. Peel the bananas and cut them in half crosswise, then again in half lengthwise. Set aside.

2. In a large sauté or frying pan over medium heat, melt the butter and brown sugar until the foam subsides.

3. Add the bananas, cut side down, to the bubbling sugar and cook for 2 minutes.

continued

4. Add the rum and light with a match to ignite the alcohol. Let the flame burn out and then add the orange juice to the pan and cook for 2 minutes more.

5. Turn the bananas over and cook another minute or two. Remove from heat.

6. To serve, spoon the bananas and the pan sauce over the ice cream.

King Cake Trifle

SERVES 6

INGREDIENTS:

2 packages instant vanilla pudding
  pudding requirement (milk)

2 cups sweetened whipped cream

1 dozen glazed donuts

2 pints raspberries (frozen are fine)

purple, green, and yellow decorating
  sugar (the colors of Mardi Gras)

1 tiny plastic baby doll

METHOD:

1. Mix the pudding according to the instructions on the package.

2. Fold the whipped cream into the pudding and set aside in the refrigerator.

3. Break the Danish pastry/donuts up into bite-size pieces.

4. Put one layer of raspberries and donuts in the bottom of a trifle bowl and top with a layer of pudding. Repeat 2 times, making 3 layers.

5. Tuck the plastic baby dolldown inside the trifle.

6. Cover the trifle and refrigerate for 2–24 hours.

7. To serve, sprinkle the purple, green, and yellow sugar on top in three separate sections.

8. Whoever gets the plastic baby doll in their serving has to host the next Mardi Gras party!

Note: You may make individual trifles in the same manner in parfait glasses and garnish each one with a plastic baby instead of hiding them inside.

Caution: Inform your guests that the plastic baby doll is not edible.

New Orleans Vocabulary

- Cajun—Nickname for Acadians, descendants from French colonists who migrated from Nova Scotia to southern Louisiana in the late 1700s

- Creole—A melding of French, Spanish, and African-Caribbean cultures found in southern Louisiana

- Crescent City—Nickname for New Orleans

- Doubloons—Gold coins tossed from carnival floats in the parades at Mardi Gras

- Juju—A charm superstitiously believed to embody magical powers

- Voodoo—A type of religion consisting of a combination of witchcraft, ancestor worship and Roman Catholic rituals originating in West Africa, coming to New Orleans by way of the Caribbean

- Zydeco—Creole Cajun folk music that is dominated by the accordion and washboard

Appalachian Dinner Show

Dolly Parton

Born in 1946 and raised in a one-room cabin in the Smoky Mountains of Tennessee, Dolly Parton scaled the hills to the summit of country music stardom early in her life and continues to remain in the rarefied air at the top—thanks to brains, beauty, talent, and a kindhearted personality. At age thirteen, Dolly was performing at the Grand Ole Opry in Nashville. The early career of the singer/songwriter flourished when she was a regular on Porter Wagoner's weekly country music television program. She would spend seven years singing on the show while recording many singles and albums. She continued to record her music after that and has received seven Grammy Awards for her work. In addition to her singing career, Dolly has had a successful acting career starting in 1980 with the movie *9 to 5*, in which she starred with Jane Fonda, followed by *The Best Little Whorehouse in Texas*, *Rhinestone*, and *Steel Magnolias*.

Dolly's fame and fortune have not jaded her, but have enabled her to spearhead programs for issues that are important to her. Her generosity and concern are evidenced in her national literacy program, Dolly Parton's Imagination Library, and her efforts to preserve the bald eagle through the American Eagle Foundation's sanctuary at her theme park, Dollywood.

Dollywood, located in her native Tennessee, is another way Dolly Parton has given back to her community, investing in the economically challenged region where she grew up. Dolly Parton's Dixie Stampede, a dinner show started at Dollywood in Pigeon Forge, Tennessee, is now in three other locations too. The restaurants at Dollywood are the inspiration for the following down-home party menu.

Dolly Parton's Smoky Mountain Shindig Comfort Food

I studied the menus for Dolly Parton's Dixie Stampede restaurants in Branson, Orlando, Myrtle Beach, and Pigeon Forge, and at the restaurants at Dollywood, and the essence is comfort; nothing fancy—just honest country cooking. Everybody needs a little comfort food now and then, so why not call up a few friends that are in need of some southern hospitality and cook them up a soul-satisfying plate of Ham Steak with Redeye Gravy? Serve it with a side of Cole Slaw and a hunk of Skillet Cornbread to sop up the gravy. Baked Apples à la Mode are a cozy end to the meal.

Ham Steak with Redeye Gravy

SERVES 4

INGREDIENTS:

2 ham steaks

2 ounces unsalted butter

¼ cup brewed coffee

½ cup boiling water

cayenne pepper sauce

pepper to taste

METHOD:

1. Melt the butter over medium high heat in a frying pan and fry the ham steaks in it, for 2 to 3 minutes on each side, or until they are browned. Transfer them to a platter and set aside in a warm oven.

2. Pour the coffee and boiling water into the same pan and cook the mixture over high heat, scraping up the browned bits, for 2 minutes.

3. Season the gravy with the hot pepper sauce and pepper and pour it over the ham steaks.

Skillet Cornbread

SERVES 8

INGREDIENTS:

2 tablespoons bacon grease

½ cup yellow cornmeal

1½ cups flour

¼ cup sugar

¼ teaspoon salt

2½ teaspoons baking powder

1 cup buttermilk

1 egg, beaten

⅓ cup oil

½ cup corn kernels

METHOD:

1. Preheat oven to 375 degrees F. Preheat a greased cast-iron skillet in the oven while preparing the mix.

2. In a bowl, combine the cornmeal, flour, sugar, salt, and baking powder.

3. In another bowl combine the buttermilk, egg, oil, and corn kernels.

4. Mix the dry ingredients with the wet ingredients and pour them into the preheated skillet.

5. Bake for 25 minutes.

6. Remove skillet from the oven and immediately invert the pan onto a cooling rack to release the cornbread from the pan.

Cole Slaw

SERVES 4

INGREDIENTS:

2 cups shredded cabbage

¼ cup shredded carrot

½ cup mayonnaise

1 tablespoon milk

1 teaspoon sugar

1 tablespoon cider vinegar

1 teaspoon celery seed

salt and pepper to taste

METHOD:

1. Mix all ingredients together.

2. Refrigerate at least 15 minutes before serving.

Baked Apples à la Mode

SERVES 4

INGREDIENTS:

4 apples, cored

⅓ cup brown sugar

2 ounces soft butter

4 teaspoons cinnamon

⅔ cup apple cider

4 scoops vanilla ice cream

METHOD:

1. Preheat oven to 350 degrees F.

2. Place the apples close together in a baking dish.

3. In a bowl, combine the brown sugar, butter, and cinnamon. Divide this mixture evenly among the 4 apples and stuff it into the holes where the cores used to be.

4. Pour the cider into the baking dish around the bottom of the apples. Cover with foil and bake the apples for 30 minutes. Uncover and baste

the apples with the liquid at the bottom of the dish and return them to the oven for 10 minutes more.

5. Remove the baked apples from the oven and serve warm with ice cream and the basting liquid drizzled over them.

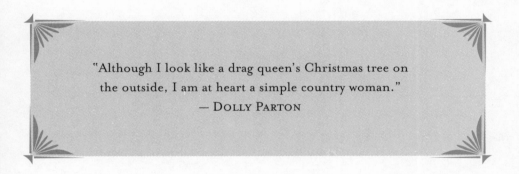

"Although I look like a drag queen's Christmas tree on the outside, I am at heart a simple country woman."
— DOLLY PARTON

Chapter 5

Political Partiers

Women Senators

What was once the sole domain of men in smoky backrooms, the United States Senate has had to date the representation of thirty-three women. The law of the land is now being shaped by Senators Barbara Boxer, Susan Collins, Dianne Feinstein, Mary Landrieu, Hillary Clinton, Blanche Lincoln, Elizabeth Dole, Barbara Mikulski, Patty Murray, Olympia Snowe, Maria Cantwell, Lisa Murkowski, Debbie Stabenow, and Kay Bailey Hutchison. Although these women make up only fourteen percent of the Senate currently, it is a long way from the days of zero percent.

The first woman to run for Senate was Mary Elizabeth Lease in 1893. She secured the nomination of the Populist Party to be its candidate for the U.S. Senate from Kansas. She lost the election, but the campaign itself was a victory. In 1922, Rebecca Latimer Felton of Georgia was the first woman to serve on the Senate. At 87 years old, she was appointed to fill a vacancy by the state's governor in a symbolic gesture designed to win women's votes for his reelection. The first woman elected to the senate was Hattie Caraway of Arkansas in 1932. She was first appointed to fill the vacancy of the seat of her husband, who had died in office, and she was subsequently voted in when a special election was held. Hattie was the first woman to preside over the Senate in 1943, and she served until 1945. When women started serving as senators they were appointed as widows to succeed their husbands' seats and then elected to complete the term, but in 1978, Nancy Kassebaum of Kansas was the first woman to run her own campaign and be elected in her own right. In 1993, Carol Moseley-Braun of Illinois became the first African-American woman ever to serve as a U.S. senator. She was one of five women elected in 1992, prompting some to call that year the "Year of the Woman." New York Senator Hillary Clinton has the distinction of having been the First Lady of the United States before she was elected in 2000. Eleanor Roosevelt would have been proud of the progress of another First Lady moving forward with her own political career.

Women of the Senate's Poker Party

What better way is there to celebrate women's success in a man's world than a poker party? But women can make wiser choices about the things they put into their bodies. For example, instead of fried potato chips and smoky cigars that traditionally accompany a card game, provide your players with healthier fare such as Poker Chips, which are actually oven-roasted vegetables, and clean-air-friendly edible Pickle Cigars. Serve your "full house" of guests Jack Stacks for snacks and prepare for a "royal flush" of compliments over this unusual version of quesadillas. "Sweeten the pot" with black and red sugar cookies shaped like hearts, diamonds, spades, and clubs. If you can't find a spade cutter (I found one at an antique store) you can at least find a heart cutter from Valentine's Day and a St. Patrick's Day shamrock to represent clubs. Diamonds can be cut with a knife or pizza wheel. If you want to add a course, "ante up" with a cup of Senate Bean Soup before the cards are dealt. I'm betting that you will find this party theme a "wild card" in your entertaining game!

Poker Chips

SERVES 4

INGREDIENTS:

2 carrots, peeled

2 parsnips, peeled

15-ounce can sliced beets, drained

6 baby red potatoes, scrubbed

½ teaspoon salt

¼ teaspoon pepper

½ cup olive oil

1 tablespoon chopped fresh rosemary

METHOD:

1. Preheat oven to 425 degrees F. Line 2 baking sheet pans (with sides) with foil and spray with baking spray.

2. Cut the carrots, parsnips, and potatoes into ⅛-inch slices.

3. Toss the carrots, parsnips, and potatoes in a bowl with ¼ cup olive oil, salt, pepper, and rosemary. Spread the vegetables out on one of the sheet pans.

4. Toss the beets in the bowl with the remaining ¼ cup of olive oil and a pinch each of salt and pepper. Spread the beets out on the other sheet pan in one layer.

5. Roast the vegetables for 20–25 minutes, or until they are crispy on the edges.

6. Let cool and then drain on paper towels.

7. Toss the chips together, put on a platter, and serve warm or at room temperature.

Jack Stacks

SERVES 4

INGREDIENTS:

1 cup diced red onion

1 cup diced mushrooms

2 tablespoons olive oil

1 ounce butter

2 tablespoons cream cheese

1 cup shredded Monterey Jack cheese

¼ teaspoon salt

¼ teaspoon pepper

2 tablespoons Parmesan cheese

12 small flour tortillas

¼ cup mayonnaise

1 tablespoon Worcestershire sauce

1 tablespoon sherry

toothpicks

METHOD:

1. Sauté the onion and mushrooms in the olive oil and butter for 15 minutes until tender. Put the cooked mixture in a bowl and stir in the cream cheese. Let the mixture cool.

2. Mix the Jack cheese, salt, pepper, and Parmesan cheese into the mushroom mixture. Spread the mixture onto 11 tortillas.

3. Stack the tortillas and top the stack with the last plain tortilla. Wrap well in plastic wrap and refrigerate 1 hour.

4. Preheat a grill or grill pan.

5. Cut the tortilla stack into ½ inch thick slices. Place a toothpick through the middle of each slice to hold the stack together and turn the slices on their sides.

6. Combine the mayonnaise, Worcestershire sauce, and sherry in a bowl.

7. Brush each slice with the mayonnaise mixture and grill 3–4 minutes a side.

8. Pull out the toothpicks before serving.

Pickle Cigars

SERVES 4

INGREDIENTS:

8 garlic dill pickles

8 thin slices Black Forest ham

4 ounces whipped cream cheese

METHOD:

1. Drain the pickles on a paper towel.

2. Spread each slice of ham with the cream cheese.

3. Roll each pickle up in a slice of ham.

Heart, Diamond, Spade, and Club Cookies

YIELD 2 DOZEN

INGREDIENTS:

4 ounces soft butter   1 egg

1 cup sugar   1 tablespoon cream   *continued*

½ teaspoon vanilla

½ teaspoon salt

1 teaspoon baking powder

1¾ cups flour

red decorating sugar

chocolate sprinkles

METHOD:

1. Preheat oven to 300 degrees F.

2. Cream the butter and sugar together until fluffy with an electric mixer.

3. Add the egg, cream, and vanilla and mix well. Scrape down the sides of the bowl.

4. In a separate bowl, mix together the salt, baking powder, and flour and then add the dry ingredients to the butter mixture. Mix to form a smooth dough.

5. Roll out the dough on a lightly floured surface. Cut out card suits with cookie cutters shaped like a heart, diamond, spade, and club.

6. Place the cut-outs on a parchment paper-lined cookie sheet.

7. Sprinkle the cut-outs alternating with the red sugar and the chocolate sprinkles.

8. Bake the cookies for 12–15 minutes. Cool the cookies before removing them from the cookie sheet.

Senate Bean Soup

A white bean soup has been on the menu in the Senate
restaurant since 1901. A good recipe for it can be found
in the classic cookbook, *The Joy of Cooking*.

Pink Poker Night

For a feminine twist on your poker game, invest in a poker set
containing pink poker chips and recipe cards designed by
Ame Mahler Beanland and Emily Miles Terry, authors of
It's a Chick Thing: Celebrating the Wild Side of Women's Friendship
In their book *Nesting: It's a Chick Thing* they lay out the way to
hold a "pink poker night" and their Pink Poker Night Kit
gives you the tools to carry it out in the right fashion.

Sunday Afternoon on the White House Lawn

First Ladies

The wives of the presidents of the United States have always been in the position of being the premier hostess in the nation. Some First Ladies have performed their duty reluctantly while others have relished the role. Some have furnished alcohol at their receptions, while others have been teetotalers. During prohibition, Florence Harding hosted poker parties in the White House library where liquor was available, even though the eighteenth amendment made it illegal. Lucy Hayes was known as "Lemonade Lucy" because she did not serve liquor at the White House, even though it was legal at that time. Mrs. Hayes's dislike of liquor did not tarnish her image though and her receptions were known to be memorable occasions. Betty Ford faced her own private battle against dependency on alcohol as First Lady and after leaving the White House she opened the Betty Ford Center to help others get treatment for this problem.

Dolley Madison was the wife of the fourth President, James Madison. Mrs. Madison is known as the woman who turned the new nation's capital, Washington, DC, from dullsville into a social scene. She served as the widowed President Jefferson's official White House hostess before her husband was elected President in 1808 and she officially became First Lady. She literally created the role as social hostess, furnishing the president's quarters and hosting weekly parties. Her lavish dinner parties were famous for their delicacies, and her knowledge of politics and current events added to her hostessing prowess. Dolley's sister got married in 1812 and hers was the first wedding to be held in the White House. In 1814, British soldiers invaded Washington and burned the president's house, but not before Dolley could save many of its valuables, including Gilbert Stuart's portrait of George Washington. A national treasure, Dolley Madison was a gracious hostess to the end, living in Washington until her death in 1849. She was so popular that her name was used as an icon for a wide range of commercial commodities, such as food, tobacco, dolls, beauty products, and other wares at the end of the 1800s.

Several First Ladies hold the distinction of having been both the wife of a President and the mother of a President. Abigail Adams was the wife of the second President of the United States, John Adams, and the mother of the sixth President, John Quincy Adams. Anna Harrison was the wife of William Henry Harrison, the first President to die in office, and the mother of twenty-second President Benjamin Harrison. Barbara Bush is the wife of George H.W. Bush and mother of George W. Bush, Presidents forty-one and forty-three. The Grande Dame of wild woman First Ladies, Eleanor Roosevelt, was a relative of two Presidents as well. She was the niece of Theodore Roosevelt and the wife of Franklin Delano Roosevelt.

The first President's wife to die in the White House was Letitia Tyler in 1842. In 1844, John Tyler remarried and became the first President to marry in office. The second Mrs. Tyler was the young, twenty-something Julia Gardiner. Frances Cleveland married bachelor President Grover Cleveland in 1886 when she was twenty-one years old, making President Cleveland the first Chief Executive to be married in the White House. Mrs. Cleveland was a popular and gracious hostess. At the time of her husband's inauguration in 1961, Jacqueline Kennedy was the youngest First Lady since Frances Cleveland. Mrs. Kennedy, another popular First Lady, led a televised tour of the White House showing its treasures. Other First Lady firsts include Lucy Hayes, who was the first presidential wife who had earned a college diploma, and Hillary Clinton, who is the first lawyer to serve as First Lady. Mrs. Clinton is also the first former First Lady to become a United States Senator.

Ice Cream Social

The role of social hostess for the nation inspired this party based on the Victorian tradition of the ice cream social. Ice cream sundaes were introduced as a way to sell ice cream sodas on Sundays without the soda, which some thought to be intoxicating. The following recipes give you a variety of choices, including Turtle Sundaes, for an ice cream get-together. Coffee Toffee Ice Cream Pie is easy to serve in precut slices, Turtle Sundaes, Banana Split Bombe is a banana split already assembled, and Tin Roof Frozen Soufflé is easily scooped.

Coffee Toffee Ice Cream Pie

SERVES 6-8

INGREDIENTS:

1 graham cracker piecrust

1 cup chopped toffee

1 quart coffee ice cream, softened

½ cup chocolate sauce

2 cups sweetened whipped cream

METHOD:

1. Sprinkle ¼ cup of the toffee on the bottom of the graham cracker crust.

2. Spread half of the coffee ice cream into the crust and smooth it out with a spatula. Sprinkle ¼ cup of the toffee on top of the ice cream and drizzle half of the chocolate sauce over it.

3. Spread the rest of the ice cream over that layer and repeat with the toffee and chocolate sauce.

4. Cover the ice cream pie with the whipped cream and sprinkle the last ¼ cup of toffee on top.

5. Put the pie in the freezer for at least 2 hours before serving.

Turtle Sundaes

SERVES 2

INGREDIENTS:

1 pint chocolate ice cream

2 ounces chocolate truffles or
   fudge, diced

¼ cup caramel sauce

¼ cup toasted pecans

½ cup sweetened whipped cream

2 pretzel twists

2 maraschino cherries

METHOD:

1. Put one scoop of ice cream in a parfait glass for each sundae.

2. Drizzle caramel sauce and sprinkle pecans and truffles/fudge over the
    ice cream.

3. Put another scoop of ice cream on top of that layer and repeat with the
    caramel sauce, pecans, and truffle/fudge.

4. Top the sundae with a dollop of whipped cream and a pretzel.

5. Drizzle caramel sauce and sprinkle pecans on top of the whipped cream.

6. Don't forget to put a cherry on top.

Banana Split Bombe

Serves 6–8

INGREDIENTS:

1 pint strawberry sorbet

½ cup sliced strawberries

2 bananas

1 pint pineapple sherbet

1 pint vanilla ice cream, softened

¼ cup grated chocolate

1 cup sweetened whipped cream

¼ cup chopped toasted almonds

8 maraschino cherries

½ cup chocolate sauce

METHOD:

1. Line a loaf pan with plastic wrap.

2. In a bowl, mix the strawberries into the strawberry sorbet and spread the mixture out in the bottom of the lined loaf pan. Place in the freezer.

3. Peel the bananas. Remove the loaf pan from the freezer.

4. Spread half of the pineapple sherbet over the strawberry layer and then put the bananas in the middle, reaching to both ends of the pan. Spread the remaining pineapple sherbet over the bananas and smooth out the layer. Return to the freezer.

continued

5. Fold the grated chocolate into the softened vanilla ice cream. Remove the loaf from the freezer again.

6. Spread the vanilla ice cream over the pineapple layer and smooth out the top. Fold the plastic wrap over onto the ice cream and return to the freezer for 2 hours to firm up.

7. After the bombe is firm, remove it from the freezer and peel the plastic off the ice cream. Lift the bombe out of the loaf pan and place it on a chilled platter, vanilla side down, and peel away the rest of the plastic.

8. Top the bombe with whipped cream, toasted almonds, and cherries.

9. Slice the bombe and serve the slices on plates with chocolate sauce.

Tin Roof Frozen Soufflé

SERVES 6

INGREDIENTS:

6 egg whites, room temperature

½ cup sugar

1 cup chopped toasted peanuts

1½ cups cream

1 ounce Amaretto

1 ounce brandy

½ cup chocolate-covered peanuts

½ cup chocolate sauce

Note: Use pasteurized eggs if you are concerned about salmonella in raw eggs.

METHOD:

1. Make a collar out of foil and tape it around the top of a 2-quart soufflé dish. Oil the dish and the collar. Set aside.

2. Whip the egg whites and gradually add the sugar until a stiff meringue forms.

3. Fold the chopped peanuts into the meringue.

4. Whip the cream to soft peaks and add the Amaretto and brandy to it.

5. Fold the whipped cream mixture into the peanut meringue mixture and turn the result into the prepared soufflé dish.

6. Sprinkle the chocolate covered peanuts over the top of the soufflé and place it in the freezer for at least 2 hours.

7. When the soufflé is firm, remove the foil collar.

8. Serve the frozen soufflé with chocolate sauce.

Presidential Suite

"You've done a nice job decorating the White House."
— singer JESSICA SIMPSON upon meeting Interior Secretary
Gale Norton at the White House

Presidential Sweets

During the 1992 Presidential campaign, Hillary Rodham Clinton's
recipe for chocolate chip cookies beat out one submitted by then-First
Lady Barbara Bush in a contest conducted by a national magazine.
Ironically, Hillary Clinton defended her choice to pursue her own
career while her husband was in political office by saying
"I suppose I could have stayed home and baked cookies."

A Depression-Era Soup Kitchen

Eleanor Roosevelt

Born a Roosevelt and married to a Roosevelt, Eleanor Roosevelt became a First Lady who changed the way First Ladies behaved. She was politically involved, held her own press conferences, and wrote a national newspaper column, "My Day." Her role as First Lady was substantial, much more than the expected position of holding teas and remaining in the background as decoration. She became a stateswoman in her own right after the death of her husband as the United States' representative to the United Nations.

Born in 1884, Eleanor grew up in a Victorian world that she eventually helped transform for women growing up in the twentieth century. She was born into a life of privilege and observed the tradition of social responsibility that women of her class felt was their duty in that day. As a young woman she volunteered at a settlement house in New York, teaching new immigrants skills to acclimate themselves and their families to American society. She exposed her future husband, Franklin, to the poverty conditions of immigrants in New York at the turn of the last century and would continue to serve as his eyes and ears, observing and reporting social conditions to him later when he became president in the midst of the Great Depression.

Social reforms became a hot topic in the Depression era and Franklin Roosevelt's New Deal made government take more responsibility in regulating the functions of society. Franklin was immobilized by polio and he relied upon Eleanor to travel the country and report on the living and working conditions in a down-and-out America. As a result of her tours of the country she was exposed to social and racial injustice and considered it her duty to use her position to influence the president to do something to correct the problems. She assisted with the Arthurdale Homestead Project for coal miners in West Virginia in 1933, she coordinated a meeting between the leader of the NAACP and the President to discuss antilynching legislation in 1934, and she arranged for African-American contralto Marian Anderson to sing at the Lincoln Memorial on Easter Sunday in 1939. Preceding the Easter event, Eleanor had resigned her membership in the Daughters of the American Revolution when they denied Marian Anderson permission to perform in Constitution Hall.

Being a civil rights, human rights, and women's rights activist made Eleanor both an admired and hated public figure in a divided America, but that never swayed her dedication. She drafted the Universal Declaration of Human Rights as the United Nations representative and later chaired President Kennedy's Commission on the Status of Women. She defied the Ku Klux Klan by speaking at a civil rights workshop in Tennessee despite their $25,000 bounty on her head, and she continued to write her "My Day" column until her death in 1962.

Soup Night

This menu is good for an informal gathering on an autumn evening, such as Election Day. You can choose one of the soups or all of them, depending on the number of people you will be feeding. Each guest can participate by hollowing out their own bread loaf or you can prepare them well in advance and stack them up on the table as part of the presentation. If you choose to make other soups that are thinner, like minestrone, provide soup cups or bowls too, since a bread bowl would get too soggy in that case. A soup night is an economical way to entertain and feed a crowd.

Hearty Beef Stew

SERVES 6

INGREDIENTS:

1 pound stewing beef cubes	1 teaspoon dried thyme
¾ cup diced onions	½ cup sliced carrots
2 tablespoons olive oil	1 potato, peeled and diced
½ cup flour	½ cup frozen peas
4 cups beef broth	1 tablespoon Worcestershire sauce
	salt and pepper to taste

METHOD:

1. Brown the beef cubes and onion in olive oil, dust meat with flour and stir to coat and distribute.

2. Add beef broth and thyme.

3. Bring to a boil then simmer for 1½ hours.

4. Add the carrots and potato and simmer for another ½ hour.

5. Add peas and season with Worcestershire sauce, salt, and pepper and simmer for 5 minutes.

Creamy Clam Chowder

SERVES 6

INGREDIENTS:

½ cup diced celery

½ cup diced onions

1 ounce butter

¼ teaspoon chopped garlic

2 tablespoons flour

1 cup clam juice

4 cups milk

3 large peeled and diced potatoes

½ teaspoon thyme

1 cup cream

1 cup drained, chopped clams

2 tablespoons chopped parsley

salt and pepper to taste

METHOD:

1. In a large pot, sauté the celery and onion in butter until translucent. Add the garlic and cook another minute.

2. Sprinkle the flour over the vegetables and cook for a minute.

3. Add the clam juice, milk, potatoes, and thyme and simmer until the potatoes are tender, about 15 minutes.

4. Add the cream, clams, and parsley and simmer for 10 minutes.

5. Season with salt and pepper.

Cheesy Broccoli Soup

SERVES 6

INGREDIENTS:

2 tablespoons butter

1 medium onion, chopped

3 tablespoons flour

½ teaspoon salt

½ teaspoon pepper

2 cups chicken broth

1½ cups chopped broccoli, fresh or frozen

2 cups milk

1 cup shredded cheddar cheese

½ cup shredded Gouda cheese

¼ cup grated Parmesan cheese

METHOD:

1. Sauté the onion in the butter until translucent in a soup pot over medium heat.

2. Sprinkle the flour, salt, and pepper over the onion and continue cooking for 2 minutes, stirring constantly.

3. Gradually add the chicken broth and then the broccoli. Bring to a boil and then cover and simmer until the broccoli is tender.

4. Add the milk and bring the soup to a simmer.

5. Stir in the cheddar and Gouda cheeses and stir over low heat just until they melt. Remove from heat.

6. Ladle the soup into bowls and sprinkle the top with Parmesan cheese.

Sourdough Bread Bowls

SERVES 6

INGREDIENTS:

6 small round sourdough loaves
  (about 5-inches diameter)

½ cup melted butter

METHOD:

1. Preheat oven to 350 degrees F.

2. Slice the top inch off each loaf to make a lid for each soup bowl.

3. Pull the bread out of the center of each bowl in chunks, leaving a 1½ inch wall around the sides and bottom of the loaves. Save the bread chunks to serve along with the soup.

4. Brush the inside of each bread bowl with melted butter and set them on two baking sheets.

5. Bake for 15 minutes, or until the inside becomes toasty.

6. Ladle soup into the bread bowls and top each with a bread lid, slightly ajar. Serve the bread chunks along with the soup bowls for dipping.

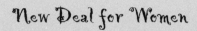
New Deal for Women

In 1932, Frances Perkins became the first woman cabinet officer for a President of the United States. She served as Franklin Delano Roosevelt's Secretary of Labor. Eleanor Roosevelt was influential in bringing about this landmark appointment.

Presidential Kids' Party

First Daughters

Being the daughter of the President of the United States is a high-profile position. Anything a First Daughter does is under the spotlight. Amy Carter, who lived in the White House from age nine to thirteen, later became known for her political activism. She was arrested, along with veteran activist Abbie Hoffman, for protesting U.S. foreign policy in South Africa and Central America in 1987, seven years after her father Jimmy Carter was no longer

President. Jenna and Barbara Bush, the First Twins, gained notoriety for incidents involving underage drinking while their father, George W. Bush, was in the White House. (Incidentally, in addition to being First Daughters, the Bush twins were also First Granddaughters when their grandfather George H.W. Bush was President.)

Teddy Roosevelt and John F. Kennedy had rambunctious young children living with them in the White House during their terms, making "normal" childhood virtually impossible for their children. Most presidential kids have not been wild, but two notable exceptions are Alice Roosevelt and Patti Davis.

Born in 1884, Alice Roosevelt was a teenager when her father, Theodore Roosevelt, became President in 1901. From the time of her debut, she was a high-profile society figure and remained in the spotlight until her death at the age of ninety-six. She was known for her independent wild streak and the media loved her. Teddy Roosevelt remarked that he "could run the country or control Alice, but he couldn't do both" in response to criticism over her lack of discipline and frequent interruptions at the White House. The presidential wild child's antics, such as smoking on the White House roof, speeding in her friend's roadster unchaperoned, and jumping into a pool fully clothed, were scandalous at the turn of the century and quite newsworthy. "Princess Alice," as she was universally dubbed, was married in the East Room of the White House and her wedding was a spectacular affair. She had a sofa pillow embroidered with feisty words that matched her attitude: "If you can't say something nice, then sit next to me." After she left the White House she continued to attract attention as a rambunctious, independent, and irreverent American social icon. Katherine Graham, the former publisher for the

Washington Post, recalled her mother telling about Alice's behavior at a party they both attended in 1920. Alice "ate three chops, told shady stories" and sang in a deep voice, 'Nobody cultivates me, I'm wild, I'm wild.'" She called herself "the other Washington monument" and lived in Washington, DC, until her death in 1980.

The same year Alice Roosevelt died, Ronald Reagan was elected President. Being politically liberal, his daughter, Patti Davis, used her mother's maiden name to distance herself from her father's conservative politics. Even before her father became President, Patti had been against his politics. In 1966, she was fourteen years old when she found out her father had been elected Governor of California and she was hysterical about it. She said "The Vietnam war was going on. Berkeley was going on . . . the one place I wanted to be . . . was on the streets of Haight-Ashbury, braiding flowers into my hair." As a teenager at that time she said that "that was her one goal in life" and she thought her father being Governor of California was terrible for her image. By the time Patti Davis became First Daughter of the U.S. she was already seen as a rebel. Her stance against nuclear weapons and her pro-choice viewpoint on abortion were in direct conflict with her father.

While her father was in office she wrote a controversial novel, *Homefront*, which included fictionalized events from her own life that did not portray her family in a positive way. President Reagan wrote in his autobiography "Patti has made it plain to me that she thinks I am wrong and she is against everything I stand for." Patti's 1992 autobiography, *The Way I See It*, furthered the rift between her and her family, with revelations that her father was cold and aloof to everyone except her mother and she made accusations of physical abuse by her mother. In 1994, at age forty-one, she posed nude for the cover of *Playboy* magazine. Ten years later, the self-described prodigal daughter stood by her family as her father slipped into the abyss of Alzheimer's. After her father's death Patti wrote, "My father belonged to the country. I resented the country at times for its demands on him, its ownership of him. America was the important child in the family, the one who got the most attention. It's strange, but now I find comfort in sharing him with an entire nation."

Pool Party

Alice Roosevelt shocked people by jumping into a pool fully clothed and Patti Davis grew up poolside in California. The renegade First Daughters' pool connection inspired this pool-centered party. A pool party is fun for kids of all ages and these recipes will help you make a big splash. Kids' favorites, such as hot dogs and hamburgers, are dressed up for a party in miniature form, and macaroni salad is made into finger food when it is served on individual lettuce leaves. The winning combination of peanut butter and bananas is paired together on a toothpick stick, lollipop fashion, for healthy, on-the-go dessert treats. Even if you only have a wading pool, you'll have fun making this pool party menu and you'll enjoy sharing it with kids or friends.

Macaroni Salad on Romaine Leaves

SERVES 6

INGREDIENTS:

2 heads of romaine lettuce

4 cups cooked macaroni

2 diced hard-boiled eggs

½ cup diced celery

1 tablespoon minced pimento

1 cup mayonnaise

¼ cup sliced green olives

2 tablespoons chopped fresh parsley

salt and pepper to taste

paprika

METHOD:

1. Wash and separate the lettuce into individual leaves. Wrap and chill.

2. Mix the macaroni, eggs, celery, pimento, mayonnaise, olives, parsley, salt, and pepper in a bowl and chill for 1 hour.

3. Arrange the lettuce leaves on a platter and put a scoop of macaroni salad on each one. Lightly dust the macaroni salad with paprika for garnish.

Hot Dogs in a Blanket

SERVES 6

INGREDIENTS:

1 sheet frozen puff pastry, thawed

1 package cocktail franks

1 egg, beaten with 1 tablespoon water

1 cup barbecue sauce

1 cup honey mustard

METHOD:

1. Preheat oven to 400 degrees F.

2. Unfold and roll the puff pastry out on a lightly floured surface to make it a little thinner.

3. Cut triangles out of the pastry big enough to wrap around the cocktail franks.

4. Wrap each cocktail frank in a pastry triangle and set them on a parchment paper-lined baking sheet pan, point side down so they won't unwrap while baking.

continued

5. Brush the egg wash on the pastry and bake for 15 minutes.

6. Serve warm with the barbecue sauce and honey mustard for dipping.

Mini Burgers

SERVES 6

INGREDIENTS:

1 pound ground beef

2 tablespoons minced onion

1 tablespoon Worcestershire sauce

¼ teaspoon celery salt

1 tablespoon Dijon mustard

¼ cup bread crumbs

¼ teaspoon pepper

½ teaspoon salt

¼ cup ketchup

18 mini bagels

Yellow mustard

Mayonnaise

2 cups shredded lettuce

5 slices American cheese,
   cut into quarters

2 thinly sliced shallots

1 cup sliced cherry tomatoes

3 baby dill pickles, sliced
   Potato Sticks (fried julienne potato
   snacks that look like miniature
   french fries and taste like potato
   chips)

METHOD:

1. Preheat oven to 350 degrees F.

2. In a bowl, combine the ground beef, minced onion, Worcestershire sauce, celery salt, Dijon mustard, bread crumbs, pepper, and salt. Form the meat mixture into 2-inch patties and place them on an oiled baking pan.

3. Brush the patties with ketchup and bake for 10-15 minutes until cooked through.

4. Slice the mini bagels in half, horizontally, and spread yellow mustard on the bottom halves and mayonnaise on the top halves.

5. Put shredded lettuce on the bottom half of each bagel.

6. Put a cooked beef patty on the lettuce and place a square of cheese on top.

7. Place a slice each of shallot, cherry tomato, and pickle on top of the cheese.

8. Place the top of the mini bagels on the mini burgers and serve on a platter. Surround the mini burgers with the potato sticks to garnish the platter.

Peanut Butter Banana Pops

Yield 6

Ingredients:

4 bananas

1 cup smooth peanut butter

¼ cup honey

½ cup crushed cornflakes

½ cup granola

toothpicks

Method:

1. Peel and cut the bananas into six chunks apiece.

2. Combine the peanut butter and honey and microwave it for 20 seconds.

3. Grind the granola in a blender or food processor for a minute, just to break it up. Mix the cornflakes with the granola.

4. Set the banana chunks out on a platter and spoon a bit of the melted peanut butter and honey over them individually.

5. Sprinkle the granola mixture over the peanut butter and place a toothpick in each banana.

Further Female Firsts

In 1968, New Yorker Shirley Chisholm became the first
African-American congresswoman in U.S. history.

In 1981, Sandra Day O'Connor was appointed by President Reagan
as the first woman to serve on the United States Supreme Court.

In 1984, Geraldine Ferraro became the first woman Vice Presidential
candidate nominated by a major political party in the United States.

In 1985, Wilma Mankiller became the first woman to
serve as the Principal Chief of the Cherokee Nation.

Acknowledgments

I would like to thank my husband Jeff and my daughter Zelda for their love and patience as I worked on this book.

Thank you to Batavia McFarlin (Mrs. B) and Izumi Kajiyama (Ms. Izumi) at the Children's Courtyard in Lewisville, Texas, for caring for my daughter.

Thank you to Brenda Knight and Jan Johnson at Red Wheel/Weiser/Conari for making this book possible. Thanks also to my wonderful editors, managing editor Caroline Pincus and copyeditor Wren Bernstein.

Thank you to my family: Mary Ellen and Fred Pilgrim, Howard Cline, Nancy Violette, Karen Cline-Parhamovich, Florence and Joseph Metzendorf, and Irene and Stanley Cline for everything that shaped me growing up.

Thank you to my great-grandmother, Katie Metzendorf, for inspiring me with her garden full of beets, peppers, and tomatoes and her kitchen full of homemade strudel, kolachi, and wax bean soup.

Thank you to Pastry Chefs Lindsey Shere and Mary Jo Thoresen, who gave me the opportunity to learn at Chez Panisse when I was a newly transplanted Buckeye in San Francisco; and Alicia Toyooka, whose perfect confections are an inspiration.

Thank you to Chef Derek Burns who took me on several culinary odysseys, including opening a restaurant on Nob Hill, running the galley of a dining yacht on San Francisco Bay, and cooking in the hallowed kitchen of James Beard in New York City.

Thank you to Casey Hayden for choosing me as a working partner for his bakery.

Thank you to fellow culinary students and caterers Meesha Halm, Nicole Alper, and Marty Stewart for their camaraderie in San Francisco.

Thank you to the Appelsmiths in Sacramento for participating in the Bag of Knives experiment.

Thank you to Jenny Boyer Howard who was my first collaborator in the kitchen (after-school snacks).

Thank you to Ken Wine for enduring my culinary awakening.

Thank you to Deacon Rohrer for many food brainstorms and dining memories.

Recipe Index

Bibliography

Beanland, Ame Mahler & Emily Miles Terry. *Nesting: It's a Chick Thing*. New York, NY: Workman, 2004.

Bolton, Lesley. *The Everything Classical Mythology Book*. Avon, MA: Adams Media, 2002.

Charlson, Carl. *Murder of the Century*. American Experience on PBS. WGBH Educational Foundation, 2003.

Dearborn, Mary V. *Mistress of Modernism: The Life of Peggy Guggenheim*. New York, NY: Houghton Mifflin, 2004.

Euripides. *The Bacchae*. New York, NY: Penguin Books, 1982.

Fisher, M.F.K. *The Art of Eating*. Hoboken, NJ: Wiley Publishing, 2004.

Fitzgerald, Peter. *Joan Crawford: The Ultimate Movie Star*. Television Documentary, 2002.

Hotchner, A. E. *Sophia Living and Loving: Her Own Story*. New York, NY: William Morrow and Co., 1979.

Lattimore, Richard. *Euripides* I. Chicago, IL: University of Chicago Press, 1955.

Lunardini, Christine Ph.D.,. *What Every American Should Know About Women's History*. Holbrook, MA: Bob Adams, Inc., 1994.

Mansfield, Stephanie. *The Richest Girl in the World: The Extravagant Life and Fast Times of Doris Duke*. New York, NY: G. P. Putnam's Sons, 1992.

Mead, Marion. *Dorothy Parker: What Fresh Hell Is This?* New York, NY: Villard Books, 1987.

Milford, Nancy. *Savage Beauty: The Life of Edna St. Vincent Millay*. New York, NY: Random House, 2001.

Milford, Nancy. *Zelda: A Biography*. New York, NY: Harper and Row, 1970.

Rubin, Nancy. American Empress: *The Life and Times of Marjorie Merriweather Post*. New York, NY: Villard Books, 1995.

Whitney, Catherine. *Nine and Counting: The Women of the Senate*. New York, NY: HarperCollins, 2000.

The Wild Women Association. *Wild Women in the Kitchen*. Berkeley, CA: Conari Press, 1996.

Williams, Sue. *Mary Pickford*. American Experience on PBS. Ambrica Productions, Inc. and WGBH Educational Foundation, 2005.

Williams, Sue. *Eleanor Roosevelt*. American Experience on PBS. PBS Online/WGBH, 1999.

www.eonline.com
www.imdb.com
www.oscars.org
www.wikipedia.org